Moving **Worlds**

...URAL WRITINGS

CW00448122

Bilangue

EDITORS:
Fiona Becket
Sam Durrant
Lynette Hunter
John McLeod
Stuart Murray
Jane Plastow
David Richards

ADVISORY BOARD
Ranjana Ash
Martin Banham
Catherine Batt
Elleke Boehmer
Erna Brodber
Romesh Gunesekera
Githa Hariharan
Salima Hashmi
Elaine Ho
John Kinsella
Koh Tai Ann
Susheila Nasta
Vincent O'Sullivan
Niyi Osundare
Nima Poovaya Smith
Anand Prahlad
Aritha van Herk

REVIEWS/BOOKS RECEIVED
Sam Durrant
WEB PAGE EDITOR
John McLeod
PRODUCTION:
Glenda Pattenden
MANAGER:
Susan Burns
EDITORIAL ASSISTANT:
Caroline Herbert

VOLUME 4 NUMBER 1 2004

Moving Worlds is a biannual international magazine. It publishes creative, critical, literary and visual texts. Contributions of unpublished material are invited. Books for notice are welcome. Manuscripts should be double-spaced with footnotes gathered at the end, and should conform to the MHRA (Modern Humanities Research Association) Style Sheet. Wherever possible the submission should be on disc (soft-ware preferably Word for Windows, Wordperfect or Macwrite saved for PC on PC formatted disc) and should be accompanied by a hard copy. Please include a short biography, address and email contact if available.

   Moving Worlds is an internationally refereed journal based at the University of Leeds. The editors do not necessarily endorse the views expressed by its contributors.

All correspondence – manuscripts, books for review, enquiries – should be sent to: The Editor, *Moving Worlds*, School of English, University of Leeds, Leeds, LS2 9JT UK

email: mworlds@leeds.ac.uk
http://www.movingworlds.net

SUBSCRIPTION RATES FOR 2004
Individuals: 1 year £25.00
Institutions: 1 year £50.00
Students: 1 year £10.00
Cheques should be made payable to: University of Leeds (Moving Worlds)
Payment is accepted by Visa or Mastercard, please contact Moving Worlds for details

Published by
Moving Worlds, at School of English
University of Leeds
Leeds
LS2 9JT UK

Copyright © 2004 *Moving Worlds*

ISBN 0 9540751 5 3   ISSN 1474-4600

Contents

Acknowledgements

Moving Worlds – Art and the Artist is published with funding assistance from the School of English, University of Leeds, and Yorkshire Arts.

We wish to thank all the contributors to this journal; to Secker & Warburg, and Vintage for use of cover illustrations to J.M. Coetzee's *Youth;* and the publishers of Abdelkebir Khatibi et Mohamed Sijelmassi, *L'art calligraphique de l'Islam,* © Editions GALLIMARD, for permission to reprint two illustrations, Adalusi-mahgribi and Kufi fleuri.

Cover illustrations:
Front. 'Terracotta Shadows', 2004, Shanaz Gulzar
Back. *From* 'Paint Pots and Strings', 2004, Shanaz Gulzar
Digitally manipulated images. Courtesy of the artist.

Translating Desire: Abdelkebir Khatibi, Calligraphy, and the *Bilangue*

DAVID RICHARDS

> Yours is the most generous Lord
> Who taught men by the pen
> That which they did not know …

Qur'an XCVI, 1-5

The standard written text of the *Qur'an* dates from the reign of Caliph Uthman (644-656). Until that point, the *Qur'an* had no earthly written form that recorded the oral recitation of the revelations which began about CE 610 and continued until Mohammed's death in CE 632. This verse epigram marks the moment in the written text when the *Qur'an* rejoices in its own textuality, self-reflexively celebrating its own revelation, its holy author, and its translation from the spoken to the written word. Since this moment, Islam and the pen have shared inseparable histories: 'Writing is an absolute, the Absolute, the *Sanctum Sanctorum*'.[1] So intertwined did they become that some Muslims made elaborate spiritual preparations for the act of writing. The Hurufi, an ancient Sufi brotherhood, for example, submitted themselves to the penetrating gaze of the sect's master until 'the word of Allah resounded deep within before appearing exoterically in the written word'. (*SIC*, p. 131)

The sacredness of the written text seems not to have been in the least tarnished by the profane nature of the materials used in its production. In the Maghreb, for example, ink was made by scorching wool from the abdomen of a sheep, pounding it with a stone, adding water to produce a paste, and heating again until dry and hard, at which point it could be mixed with water to make a black or brown ink (*SIC*, p. 75). Usually the pen was a simple reed which the scribe would taper and divide at the point in order to hold the ink, but it was believed that 'the tip of the pen is what marks the difference between cultures' (*SIC*, p. 14), so it was cut square or bevelled depending on the choice of script – *naskhi* or *thuluth* – or the kind of calligram – *bismillah* or *tugruth* – to be written. But, for special purposes and other occasions, different kinds of pens could be fashioned. A message of friendship was written with a pen made from a stork's beak; a pomegranate branch was used for communicating with an enemy; a pen of red copper was used to inscribe a marriage contract on wax (*SIC*, p. 100). Writing, particularly in its most refined form in the high art of sacred calligraphy, was a pursuit of the great as well as the métier of the lowly scribe. To mention one example, the Vizier Ibn Muqla (886-940) combined a passion for calligraphy with a love of gardens (where he hung nests of silken threads in the trees to attract birds); and as well as hatching plots against the Abbasid Caliph Radi Billah (who cut off his tongue, his right hand, and sentenced him to life imprisonment), Ibn Muqla is credited with the invention of *naskhi*, the geometric codification of the cursive style of writing, which he perfected with his left hand (*SIC*, p. 101).

As a copyist working from pre-existing texts, the calligrapher's role is akin to that of the translator. The art resides in the successful reconciliation of two opposed ambitions: to craft a text that is both a faithful reproduction and a significant transformation of the original. Like a translated text, calligraphy exists in the interstices of the source text and a wholly new creation, and its most successful realizations produce a state of indeterminacy in the viewer, who is forced to engage in simultaneous acts of reading and looking:

> Calligraphy derives its strength from the act of reading, and that of looking without reading. There is at all times an imbalance between the two, a displacement, a scansion and a loss of meaning. That is why a piece of calligraphy may be considered a picture in process of developing from its original conception. It opens the way to another stage of reading, that of the writer, who searches continually for an emotional and perceptional rhythm for the written structure that he strives to create. (*SIC*, p. 214)

The calligrapher's purpose is to alter the written sign so that the 'noiseless musical quality of the text as a whole', 'the readable and the elusive, the impression of what one sees and the presence of the voice' is rendered by his art 'in the form of light and shade' (*SIC*, p. 6). By treating language simultaneously as lexis and plastic form, calligraphy resides between image and meaning. And, while active at the 'edge of language', calligraphy is nonetheless wholly consistent with the Arabic rhetorical practice of *al-Adab*, which, rejecting the 'primacy of any single system' associated with science, literature, or education, subtly and simultaneously draws on multiple rhetorical strategies 'delicately veiled for our greater enjoyment' (*SIC*, p. 23).

Abdelkebir Khatibi, the Maghrebine novelist, sociologist, philosopher,

Fragment of a page from the Qur'an:
Andalusian maghribi script on coloured silk
in *L'art calligraphique de l'Islam*
© Editions GALLIMARD

and historian of calligraphy, from whose work these quotations are taken, sees calligraphy as an expression of *al-Adab* and as a model for his own writings. Just as he maps his own theories of cultural difference and exchange, writing, reading, and 'looking' onto the translational ideal of calligraphic art, so calligraphy denotes for Khatibi 'an all-embracing cultural manifestation which structures the philosophical basis of regular language' (*SIC*, p. 15). The exemplary object calligraphy produces has a double existence as visual spectacle and as textual entity, and they exist in a perpetual state of 'translation' whereby something, and (by extension) someone, is forever in the process of 'being translated'. Like the rhythmical horizontal lines of Arabic script from which the cursive line departs in arabesques and parabolas, his own texts weave similar 'calligraphic' patterns between language *in situ* and language *in actu*.[2] His dominant rhetorical motif, as McNeece and Beebee have observed, is the figure of the cursive arc of Arabic script – the 'parabola' which is reproduced in the patterns of his novels' language and structure and which attempts to 'open the way to another stage of reading', disturbing the 'course of the text' by revealing that 'meaning is a sort of optical illusion, skimming across a celestial prism'.[3]

Khatibi's novel *Amour bilingue* (*Love in two languages*) tells a simple tale of love between a Maghrebine man and a European woman; such a simple tale that the narrator tells it all in the first line between parentheses: '(He left, he came back, he left again. He decided to leave for good. The story should stop here, the book close upon itself.)'[4] Almost all there is of the novel's narrative is contained in these brackets; however, the book does not 'close upon itself', indeed it remains open for another 130 pages. In fact the temporal sequence this prefaced summary suggests is entirely absent from the rest of the novel since Khatibi postpones any sense of a linear progression of events as he weaves a complex textual web of mystical references, journeys, genres, and languages. Similarly, the treatment of character breaches any conventional apprehension of individuality as the lovers merge with each other, with the landscapes, and, increasingly, with the different languages they speak to the point that they become merely the vessels of their mutual acts of translation.

> At the beginning, it was totally confusing. Around her, one language was spoken, then another, and occasionally the languages were mixed together, feverishly. In fact, no language decided to impose itself, to be the higher law, to always play the leading role. A scene played out secretly, where what was hidden in me, my suffering, appeared in separate acts, and, so to speak, without major consistence. (*L*, p. 79)

Translation acts like desire as language and the body are suffused in their yearning to translate themselves into each other. This language of love is indistinguishable from the love of language which 'obliterates time and eternity' and becomes 'plurilangue, mad thought and unmeasurable desire' (L, p. 81). Telling his story, the narrator 'imagined himself to be a detour of a being, an emotive disjuncture of the language, one voice among many. Yes, he imagined himself to be a simple progression, whose progress was in no way guaranteed; thoughts so minimal, so fragile' (L, p. 38). The text traces flamboyant arcs and loops, replicating a 'trans-rhetorical', al-Adab, or 'calligraphic' narrative; and adorns its thin central movement with cursive parabolas of linguistic desire and dissolving identities.

As Abdellah Mdarhri-Alaoui has it, 'Khatibi's texts write themselves, in a continuous mirroring, from the inside out and from the outside in'; and what the reader experiences is 'an endless displacement of the story and ... a continuous mutation of its dominant references'.[5] Not surprisingly, Amour bilingue is a text which defies categorization, as Khatibi himself admits: 'If I were asked, is your story a new nouveau roman? Or, better, a bi-novel new novel? I'd reply that the novel never had any affection for me. We don't have the same history.' (L, p. 115) Khatibi's disavowal of the novel directs his reader to an alternative 'history' as his narrative style attempts to endow the text with the parabolic qualities of Arabic script by drawing out the 'calligraphic' properties of the processes of translation. Those processes become most intense and productive when the acts for translation become distracted and lead him on unexpected detours. Detours such as when translating the word 'flower' to nouar conjures up a double meaning in the Arabic word of both flower and syphilis; or when the narrator remembers that Fitna is a homograph in Arabic for both 'war' and 'seduction'; or when musing on the closeness in French of mot ('word') to mort ('death'),

> an Arabic word, kalma, appeared, kalma and its scholarly equivalent, kalima, and the whole string of its diminutives which had been the riddles of his childhood: klima. ... The diglossal kal(i)ma appeared again without mot's having faded away or disappeared. Within him, both words were observing each other, preceding what had now become the rapid emergence of memories, fragments of words, onomato-poeias, garlands of phrases, intertwined to the death: undecipherable. (L, p. 4)

This is not the practice of translation in any conventional sense – one in which the act of translation is invisible and erases itself in the process of crossing languages. Nothing is actually translated here: 'mot' is not decoded into its Arabic equivalent or alternative, 'kalima'. Instead,

Khatibi both links and holds apart these words as they gaze at each other across languages and cultures. Translation in this sense is not the transportation of the source text into another linguistic system or into the cultures of these words, but the elaboration and celebration of the 'irresolution' (as Walter Benjamin described it) of translation's perpetually incomplete processes.[6] Khatibi claims that 'translation' is better described as 'transmutation' (L, p. 60) as the reader is drawn by this process into a movement of another kind – from 'word' to 'death', to 'calm', to 'word', to childhood memories – and at each stage in the 'calligraphic arc' of the linguistic parabola, the trace of the previous word is carried into the next. The focus of Khatibi's attention is neither the source word nor its various transformations, but the mysterious linkages and dreamlike passages between them.

In trying to get closer to Khatibi's meaning, I'm reminded of a story a friend used to tell against himself. A brilliant historian and linguist, my friend was, nonetheless, a very boring lecturer who could send an entire lecture hall of students to sleep. On one occasion, he claimed to have sent himself to sleep. Having dozed off speaking in English, he woke up moments later and continued in German, without being aware that he'd 'translated' himself. Khatibi, it can be said, is absorbed by what happens in the 'sleep' between those two moments of different linguistic lucidity. Or, more to the point, 'what was it like to dream in the two languages simultaneously?' (L, p. 10). These dreamlike transitional/translational states Khatibi calls the *bilangue*.[7] The *bilangue* is a key term in Khatibi's lexicon, referring not only to the linguistic contexts of translation, which it suggests, but to the whole range of similar themes and practices which inform his thinking – calligraphy, the cursive parabola, *al-Adab* – and upon which he constructs his cultural politics. The *bilangue* exists only in these various processes of translation (conceived in the wider *allusive* sense) and is obliterated by and is opposed to translation (conceived in the narrower *conclusive* sense), the goal of which is invisibility, closure, and substitution. Just as calligraphy exists between text and image, or as desire 'interinanimates' the bodies of the lovers, so the *bilangue* inhabits a place between the languages which have engendered it. The *bilangue* secretes itself in language; it is the desire of language to translate itself.

Khatibi's ideas of the *bilangue* and translation as transmutation, and their radical difference from conventional notions of discrete monolingual domains and from translation as 'transportation', form the foundations of his cultural politics; cultural politics which arise also from his disputes with current theories on the postcolonial condition and from his insights into the distinctiveness of Maghrebine cultures. The Maghreb is a significant location in contemporary poststructuralist debates, not least because many of the theorists who occupy central positions in those debates – Sartre, Althusser, Derrida, Lyotard, Fanon, Memmi, Bourdieu, Cixous – were closely associated with the Maghreb, were either born there, lived there, carried out important research there, or were engaged in Maghrebine politics. The Maghreb is therefore an influential location in postcolonial modernity. One such significant moment in the Maghrebine formation of postcolonialism is evoked by Homi Bhabha, who fixes upon Roland Barthes's description of himself in *Pleasure of the Text*, 'half-asleep on his banquette in a bar' in Tangiers, and attempting to '"enumerate the stereophony of languages within earshot": music, conversations, chairs, glasses, Arabic, French':

> Suddenly the inner speech of the writer turns into the exorbitant space of the Moroccan souk:
> [T]hrough me passed words, syntagms, bits of formulae and no sentence formed, as though that were the law of such a language. This speech at once very cultural and very savage, was above all lexical, sporadic; it set up in me, through its apparent flow, a definitive discontinuity: this non-sentence was in no way something that could not have acceded to the sentence, that might have been before the sentence; it was: what is ... *outside the sentence.*[8]

Against Barthes's image of Tangiers, Bhabha (without commenting on its appalling orientalist tendencies) erects the counterpoint of Casablanca, as depicted in the famous film starring Humphrey Bogart, and the song which Sam the pianist is repeatedly asked to play. 'In Casablanca, the passage of time preserves the identity of language; the possibility of naming over time is fixed in the repetition.'[9] The Maghreb is either Casablanca, locked in the dull compulsion to repeat and fix meaning, or Tangiers, with its fluid incoherence outside meaning.

Barthes's experiences in Tangiers represent a significant moment in Bhabha's influential construction of postcolonialism, because of its powerful evocation of a cacophony of hybrid tongues forcing themselves into audibility from the margins of Western consciousness. The polyglot flow of languages, irregular and volatile, marks the Maghreb as the 'exemplary' location of Bhabha's postcolonial culture. The Maghrebine genealogy of postcolonial critique is further strengthened by another French intellectual in another 'exemplary' Maghrebine location. For Robert Young, postcolonialism emerged out of Jacques Derrida's Algerian origins and his consequent determination to deconstruct 'force and its traces in language … and above all history as violence, ontological, ethical and conceptual violence'.[10] For Young, Derrida has contributed immeasurably to the constitution of the postcolonial subject by his analyses of 'the excluded other', 'the operations of reason', 'inside/outside structures', 'alterity', 'difference', 'displacement', 'the destabilizing encroachment of the marginal', 'the subversive subaltern', and 'the constitutive dependency of the centre on the marginal'.[11] But Young goes further, in that he finds in the figure of Derrida himself the archetype and very essence of the postcolonial subject. Derrida, the exiled North African Jew, uniquely occupies a position of multiple differences and colonizations which cluster around and perpetually inform his work. Nowhere is this more apparent than in his relationship to language: 'I love words too much because I have no language of my own.'[12] In *Le monolinguisme de l'autre*, Derrida recounts the history of the Algerian Jews from the 1870 Cremieux laws to their fate under the Vichy regime (the first granted Jews citizenship, the second stripped them of their legal status) within the linguistic paradox of his own biography. The text is prefaced by a statement which determines the content of the rest of the book: 'I have only one language. It isn't mine.'[13] 'Deprived of all language, inhabiting only foreign languages … without a source language', Derrida is depicted and depicts himself as 'encrypted inside a stranger's language that was not [his] own, making [him] a stranger to [him]self'.[14]

The exemplary site of Barthes's Tangiers and the equally exemplary figure of the displaced, de-languaged, deconstructive Maghrebine philosopher would seem to converge in Khatibi's writings also. Certainly, Khatibi's *bilangue* would be more at home in Tangiers than Casablanca, with his own characterizations of Maghrebine 'inner speech' taking on the tones of the 'exorbitant space of the Moroccan souk'. Similarly, *Amour bilingue* would appear to exist in a comparable condition of Derridean postcoloniality, in continuous encryptions of translation/transmutation, both in and between languages and cultures:

> … if the thing within me is in the order of the unnameable and if, for its own benefit, the unnameable transforms itself in the fiction of the always-known which will have gone ahead of me, into what transparency was I projected? Was I, in these moments, wandering in a universe which was not, which is neither thing nor name, but rather a kind of drunken forgetting, where my ordeal turned into an empty exaltation? What was I without language, my master? (*L*, p. 80)

Khatibi's own insistence that his writings require 'a double figure of reading', and are a 'disjuncture of the language', a 'language which only half understands me' would seem to suggest that Khatibi and Derrida are subject to the same linguistic regime, lending weight to the often repeated critical perception of Khatibi, that his work represents a 'decolonization of the Maghreb from French … domination, a textual decolonization carried out from within, with the help of Deconstruction'.[15]

Yet, in response to Derrida's statement in *Le monolinguisme de l'autre* ('I have only one language. It isn't mine'), which quintessentially defines Derrida as *the* postcolonial subject for subsequent postcolonial theorists, Khatibi replies by excavating the histories of the various languages spoken by Judeo-Maghrebians. Judeo-Arabic, Hakitiya, and Berber are all languages which Jews share with Maghrebine Arabs and Berbers. Far from having 'only one language', Jews in the Maghreb have many languages, and Derrida's exclusive and excluded monolingualism makes him, not an exemplar of the Maghrebine postcolonial condition, but a singular exception in the Maghreb. Derrida sees his own linguistic delimitation and colonization as a universal condition of the postcolonial, whereas Khatibi depicts Derrida as being atypical of both Maghrebine Jews and Arabs who share many languages. According to Khatibi, Derrida clings to the misapprehension that one can own a language – an extraordinary proposition for a critic of Western logocentricism.[16] Further, deconstruction's critique presents *one* Western language (French) as language *per se*, which leads Derrida to replicate and perpetuate the fundamental underpinnings of colonial language while masquerading as a radical critic of linguistic colonization. Khatibi's alternative to the genealogies of deconstruction involves, what he calls, '*pensée autre*', 'an other thinking'; the ability to think outside the dichotomies which emerge from deconstruction's critique of colonial language.[17] Khatibi's anti-colonial strategies seek to eschew oppositional conceptions by locating his writing in the uncertain, 'unnameable' domains of desire, the *bilangue*, and translation/transmutation, but '*pensée autre*' also has, at its root, a calligraphic character and history.

Orientalist historians of calligraphy attach extraordinary significance to the two dominant types of Arabic script: 'an angular, geometric script of a hieratic and monumental nature, used originally to transcribe the *Qur'an* or texts of great religious or literary value; and a rounded cursive script employed by scribes for everyday documents. It … became customary to designate the early script as '*kufic*', the cursive type as '*naskhi*' (*SIC*, p. 96). In 'orientalist theory', the distinctions between the types of script have ideological significance as evidence of an 'antithesis

of sacred and profane: the contrast of religious morality secularized in the rationalism of epigraphy' (*SIC*, p. 98). Ibn Muqla's invention of *naskhi* therefore represents much more than a 'geometric codification ... according to Euclidean theory' (*SIC*, p. 97); it is an ancient and subversive liberalism within Islam, an alternative to the rigid theocracy represented by *kufic* script.

Yet to Khatibi, this dichotomy which is perceived to exist within Arabic calligraphy says more about the distortions of orientalism than the facts of Islamic history.

> [*T*]*he two scripts evolved in parallel.* And through the codification of the *khat al-mansub* (proportioned writing), Ibn Muqla reformed Arabic calligraphy from *naskhi* and not from *kufic*. The predominance of the former never led to the elimination of the latter. The remarkable continuity of their coexistence is rooted in the culture of Islam, in its different manifestations. (*SIC*, p. 98)

His insistence that *naskhi* evolved stylistically from pre-existing cursive scripts rather than as an antagonistic response to theocratic *kufic* is more significant than it appears at first sight. His argument undermines the orientalist subtext that Islam is a monolithic repressive orthodoxy which suppresses its followers to the point that its recalcitrant opponents adopt alternative, dissident scripts. As in his writings on the history of the languages of Maghrebine Jews, Arabic calligraphy reveals a history of multiple cultural translations and 'irresolutions': an infinitely more complex model of the Maghrebine inheritance than either orientalism or deconstruction has allowed. But this is not to suggest that Khatibi is an apologist for Islam; on the contrary, his writings contain frequent acerbic comments on the repressive role of Islamic theocracies, particularly in the Maghreb. For him, the 'theological unity between the city of God and the city of men ... is deadly. It is identified with a model of civilization that is no longer viable while the world in a state of becoming obeys a new language, experimental and exploratory'. He condemns religion for delivering 'the soul of the believer to the anguish of the invisible'.[18] He disputes that the *Qur'an* demands the blind obedience of its adherents, arguing instead that the holy text encourages critical engagement:

> Recall the first words revealed to the Prophet Muhammad, 'Read, recite.' Does not the word *Qur'an* also mean the act of reading and recitation? Read the world and the heavens as a table of signs. You are first and foremost a reader, then a believer. (*SIC*, p. 6)

Khatibi's writings on calligraphy resonate with his wider theories of '*pensée autre*'. Although he nowhere refers to Homi Bhabha's postcolonial dialectic, it is analogously recalled in this demolition of orientalist history of calligraphy; it is not simply a matter of polarized cultural paradigms – *naskhi* or *kufic*, 'Tangiers' or 'Casablanca' – but of something much more deeply interfused, something more *bilangue*. The Orientalists' Islamic subject is placed between *naskhi* and *kufic*, repression and resistance. The Derridean postcolonial subject is placed between language and silence, binary frames of identity, enduring the 'rupture' and 'dissonance' of the 'the language of the other'. Ironically the latter has similar pretensions to global relevance as the former, sustaining the colonial habit of dichotomous thinking while claiming nonetheless to be its most radical critic. For Khatibi, these are *manifestations of difference* rather than something more deeply 'rooted in the culture of Islam, in its *different manifestations*' (*SIC*, p. 98). '*Pensée autre*' offers a way to think beyond those questions of identity by disputing the binary formulations which preserve the Manichean structures of 'difference'.

'*Pensée autre*' and the *bilangue* aren't abstruse theoretical models in the polyglot 'translated' Maghrebine social world: the novelist Fouad Laroui has described the 'stereophony of languages', in more vital terms than Bhabha and Barthes, as a 'ratatouille of words', neither 'very cultural and very savage' nor 'exorbitant' and certainly 'not outside the sentence'.[19] In Khatibi's diurnal *Maghreb pluriel*, such matters as translation, transmutation, and the *bilangue* are commonplace; 'the language of the other' is 'dissonance' and 'rupture' but it is also a 'point of suture'.[20] His answer to his own question – 'What was I without language?' – is neither the Derridean '*étranger clandestin*' nor Barthean 'incoherence': Khatibi's 'task is to implacably translate its emotional power' (p. 86). Finally, it needs to be noted that, in erecting a dichotomy which is useful to his argument, Bhabha passes over the geopolitical and historical location of the Maghreb as being insignificant: 'Tangiers' and 'Casablanca' could be anywhere, are everywhere, because we're all postcolonial now. But the Maghreb isn't just anywhere; it is a unique location. As Walter Mignolo (with many others) has argued, 'located between Orient, Occident, and Africa … [it] is a crossing of the global in itself'.[21] The Maghreb is one of those spaces which, 'like memory, is in the process of becoming', enunciated in, rather than obscured by, its 'stereophony of languages', translations, sacred texts, calligraphic arabesques, Sufi rituals, and deconstructive narratives. Its guiding spirit is a one-handed calligrapher – the Vizier who turned burnt wool into the calligram which is the mirror of Allah.

NOTES

1. A. Khatibi and M. Sijelmassi, *The Splendour of Islamic Calligraphy* (London: Thames and Hudson, 1995), p 22. All further references are to this edition and given in the text as *SIC* followed by the page number.
2. The phrases *in situ* and *in actu* in relation to language and translation are taken from Homi K. Bhabha, *The location of culture* (London: Routledge, 1994), p. 228.
3. T.O. Beebee, 'The Fiction of Translation: Abdelkebir Khatibi's *Love in Two Languages*', *Sub-Stance*, 73 (1994) 69; L.S. McNeece, 'Decolonizing the sign: Language and Identity in Abdelkebir Khatibi's *La memoire tatouee*', *Yale French Studies*, 83:2 (1993) 25; Khatibi and Sijelmassi, *The Splendour of Islamic Calligraphy*, p. 91.
4. A. Khatibi, *Love in two languages*, translated by Richard Howard (Minneapolis: University of Minnesota Press, 1990), p. 3. All further references are to this edition and given in the text as *L* followed by the page number.
5. A. Mdarhri-Alaoui, 'Abdelkebir Khatibi: Writing a Dynamic Identity', *Research in African Literatures*, 23:2 (1992) 169.
6. On the example cited here ('*mot*' – '*mort*' – '*kalma*' – '*kalima*'), see Beebee, 'The Fiction of Translation', 67-9; also W. Benjamin, *Illuminations: Essays and Reflections*, ed., H. Arendt (New York: Schocken., 1968), p. 75; Bhabha, *The location of culture*, p. 228; F. Cheng and A. Khatibi, *Abdelkebir Khatibi* (Rabat: Okad, 1990); J McGuire, 'Forked Tongues, Marginal Bodies: Writing as Translation in Khatibi', *Research in African Literatures*, 23:1 (1992); A. Mdarhri-Alaoui, 'Abdelkebir Khatibi: Writing a Dynamic Identity', *Research in African Literatures*, 23:2 (1992); W. Mignolo, *Local histories/global designs: coloniality, subaltern knowledges, and border thinking* (Princeton: Princeton University Press, 2000).
7. *Bilangue* is a word of Khatibi's own coinage and is related to, but distinct from, the adjective *bilingue* (meaning 'bilingual') and the noun *langue* (meaning variously 'tongue', 'language', and 'way of speaking').
8. Bhabha, *The location of culture*, p. 180.
9. Bhabha, *The location of culture*, p. 182.
10. Robert Young, *Postcolonialism: an historical introduction* (Oxford: Blackwell, 2001), p. 418.
11. Young, *Postcolonialism*, p. 418.
12. Geoffrey Bennington and Jacques Derrida, *Jacques Derrida* (Chicago: University of Chicago Press, 1993), pp. 92-93.
13. J. Derrida, *Monolingualism of the other, or, the prosthesis of origin* (Stanford, Calif: Stanford University Press, 1998); see also R. Scharfman, 'La langue de l'autre', *Research in African Literatures*, 33:1 (2002) 192.
14. Young, *Postcolonialism*, p. 423.
15. Beebee, 'The Fiction of Translation', 73-74.
16. A. Khatibi, *La langue de l'autre* (Saratoga Springs, NY: Les Mains Secretes, Centre d'Etudes sur les Litteratures d'Afrique du Nord, 1999); see also R. Scharfman, 'La langue de l'autre', *Research in African Literatures*, 33:1 (2002) 192-193.
17. See B. Aresu, 'Introduction', *Sub-Stance*, 69 (1992); R. Bensmaia, 'Writing Metafiction: Khatibi's *Le Livre du Sang*', *Sub-Stance*, 69 (1992); Mignolo, *Local histories/global designs*.
18. A. Khatibi, 'A Colonial Labyrinth', *Yale French Studies*, 2:83 (1993) 9-10.
19. M. Rosello, 'De la bilangue de Khatibi a la langue amere de Fouad Laroui: *Amour bilingue* ou *Mefiez-vous des parachutistes*', *Presence francophone*, 55 (2000).
20. 'Se fier a la langue de l'autre est bien a la fois un point de suture et de rupture, sinon de dissidence.' Khatibi cited in Scharfman, 'La langue de l'autre', 192-193.
21. Mignolo, *Local histories/global designs*, p. 69.

ADAM STRICKSON

Five Boards Waiting

It's true, the simplest things
last, like trades or undone business.

We'd been talking wood, the linen boxes,
how wood becomes jewels and miracles
when all the trees are gone, how wood is
hidden in the blood, how wood is a dance.

There'd been a catalogue of deaths:
the end of piano duets, a coma in Crete,
a slip from a cliff rope, two cancers.

★

Five boards, he said. *Five boards —*
I sent them to the wheelwright Chipping Norton way,
told him to use copper nails. That way I'll last longer.

He'd stepped out of 'The Norman Knight'
the day before the dance, on his way to ninety,
curry sauce stains on his shirt of old man blue,
drips in his white beard, goose grass on his cuff
but still sharp, still the thing we're all after.

I've had the best crop of wheat ever so I sent
five boards — one extra, just in case.
It's thirty years since I cut down the oak.
It was in the way. You couldn't do that now.

I knew him as a singer first, farmer second.
I knew him when he told his wife to scarper,
took up with his secretary, kept things tax efficient.

I'm still a working farmer, born in those trees.
I've built my land piece by piece. My grandad
was a farm worker. I'm worth three million,
still a working farmer, so no inheritance tax.

A man in both sheep and arable, a hare
who can see what lies around the bend.

I'd like, he said, *some nice requiems.*
I'd like, he said, *some Handel or Verdi:*
there's plenty of money in the kitty.

Wool from these hills was carried
to the high, rose cities of Italy. The woolpacks
carried jewels and miracles, the thing
they were all after, the Gloucester fleece.

It was, he said, *the softest in the world.*
It was, he said, *the gold that built the churches,*
the gold which bought the merchants of Campden
some nice requiems.

He's off to America, to stay with a daughter

I'll get my fiddle down from the loft.
I've got cats for strings, a horse for the bow.
I'll play a tune, fiddle my way towards those
five boards. Tomorrow, I'll dance on the Green.

He has no undone business to speak of.

Stratford Biology

You found them in the backroom, sent to wash out a pipette.

You knew those two addled, pickled eggs with webbed hands,
sealed in brown glass, were two might-have-been-children,
who guarded between them, a skull, a dirty thing with teeth.

They sat, eating their own tails, on the shelves above
owl pellets, claws, carapaces, winged bones and eyeballs.

You knew this flesh and bone was out of place, vaguely illegal.

You stared at the folded crinkles of two underwater cheeses,
worried by their closed eyes, unconvinced by their quietness.
You tipped the edge of one jar, watched the still life judder
and failed to connect it with a cloudy act under a car blanket
by someone in gingham, and someone in winklepickers.

You found the skull easier, closer to sketched rabbit bones
with its cracks like grubby fingernails and hard after-life.

You picked it up like a fumbling Dad with his newborn
and pushed aside the sniggered whisper of 'Alas…'
with 'Blest be he that spares these bones', engraved
beneath Shakespeare's stone belly in the church:
the verger told you his bones had gone down river,
washed out by floods slip-slapping the chancel floor.

You looked up at the two unswimming whitenesses,
thought of the weighty burgher, slumped over his desk,
dying, crying for his lost son, Hamnet, twin brother of Judith,
but couldn't give names to lives without birth, without death.

Memory, Gender, and National Identity in the Work of Assia Djebar

When she was asked by a journalist, 'Why do you write?', Assia Djebar replied, 'I write to break my silence.' She then added, 'to confront and fight two kinds of silence, one of which is my own, while the second is that of Muslim women who are often denied a voice.'[1] By taking this approach, Djebar commits herself to *writing silence*, an endeavour which has been the backbone of her literary work. Throughout her novels, short stories, films, poetry, and what is to date her only play, she records the suppressed voices of women from various strata of society, and gives her characters and her own '*self*' the opportunity to utter words they cannot or are not allowed to say in real life. In so doing, she transforms silence into non-silence, and makes the invisible visible.[2]

Assia Djebar's first novel, *La Soif*,[3] depicts the predicament of Nadia, a young girl who, like the author when she wrote the novel, is twenty years old. Of mixed descent, Nadia looks more French than Algerian, and aspires to the lifestyle typical of the European girls in her city. She does not have to face the constraints imposed on her Algerian sisters in a society opposed to the emancipation of women, yet she constantly suffers from a feeling of emptiness that is given vivid expression in her ardent search for pleasure. It causes her to break her engagement with her fiancé and encourage the attentions of Hassein. Through the eyes of her protagonist, Djebar examines the relationship between the sexes, a topic that is to become a typical feature of her later work. Nadia's curiosity draws her towards Jedla and Ali, whom she sees as an ideal couple. However, the more she becomes involved in their lives, the more she learns that their happiness is a façade. Unhappy as she is, Jedla tries to take her own life. Instead of helping her out of her crisis, Nadia condemns her for her selfishness, and becomes attracted to Ali on account of his calm personality and his looks. Aware of this, and feeling increasingly insecure, Jedla offers her handsome husband to Nadia, and sinks into acute depression after the miscarriage of her baby. Deeply humiliated by Jedla's offer, Nadia finds herself at a loss. Does she really

moving worlds 4.1　　　　　　　　　　　　　　　　**17**

want Ali? Or does she prefer Hassein, who knows her well and is capable of confronting her with the truth about herself: 'I know you. You need men at your feet even if you do not like them ... You are thirsty for men' (pp. 84-85). Nadia does not refute Hassein's statement, though she knows her thirst is not solely for men but for self-discovery, freedom, and pleasure as well.

Although the French press praised *La Soif*, which they likened to Françoise Sagan's *Bonjour tristesse*, Djebar met with bitter criticism from the Algerian nationalist intelligentsia, who accused her of writing about a reality completely alien to Algerian society. They found it indecent that the author was writing about sexual problems at a time when her fellow Algerians were fighting for the liberation of their country. The 1950s are known as a decade when the Algerian novel was dominated by political commitment:

> With the outbreak of the Algerian war of independence, those who were demanding that writers commit themselves and their work totally to the national cause became increasingly vocal. At its congress held in Algeria on the 20th of August 1956, the F.L.N. insisted that Algerian literature should be dedicated to praising the heroic struggle for national independence.[4]

In essence, what the nationalist critics were calling for was propagandist literature. They did not seem to understand the difference between a novel and a *témoignage*. Novelists like Mouloud Mammeri and Mouloud Feraoun resisted these pressures, and held that bearing witness to their people's dilemmas was a form of commitment. Djebar however disowned *La Soif*, claiming that she did not take her novel seriously and that she herself was not serious about the subject at all. Forty years later, Assia Djebar looked back at *La Soif* and admitted that what she had written in this novel was what she had wanted to write. At the age of twenty, she was seeking a way of expressing her dreams. Writing was a way for the young Algerian student she then was to escape the pressures of her life, just as later it became a refuge from her silence as an exiled woman.[5] One critic who understood Djebar's quest in *La Soif* was Abdelkabir Khatibi, whose book *Le Roman Maghrebin* asked: 'Have we really understood that the discovery of the body for the character of *La Soif* is also an important revolution ?'[6]

In the 1950s, Djebar's reply to the nationalist critics was her second novel *Les Impatients* which she set in the summer prior to the 1954 revolution.[7] The central character, a young woman of eighteen, belongs to a traditional family for whom the word honour is of the greatest significance and whose main concern, having lost its wealth over the years, is to maintain the prestige of their family name. Dalila's struggle for freedom from the constraints and dictates of her sheltered existence takes a familiar form. Rebelling against those appointed to be her guardians, her brother and her stepmother, she pursues love and her relationship with Salim for the opportunities they seem to hold out for the individual's right to personal feelings and expression. Unfortunately Salim turns out to be incapable of understanding her predicament and her desire to escape the trappings of a rigid, hypocritical society. After much confusion and uncertainty, Dalila, now in France to attend university, decides it is time to break free again.

In *La Soif* and *Les Impatients*, Djebar's young protagonists are among the lucky few to have had access to education during the 1940s, and who have been instilled with an awareness of their personal condition through education. Their alienation is not portrayed as a result of colonialism as in the works of other contemporary Algerian writers.[8] Before becoming involved in the quest for national identity through their participation in the war for independence, Djebar's characters have to undertake a quest for personal identity. Both Nadia and Dalila, as we have seen, are in search of a feminine self, denied to women in a patriarchal society. However, one lesson the quest for self-discovery brings to Djebar's heroes and heroines is that a person cannot achieve freedom if his/her country is not free. Djebar calls these characters 'children of the new world', from which she takes the title of her third novel.

Unlike the earlier novels which are first-person narratives, *Les Enfants du nouveau monde* is narrated in the third person and follows a large collection of characters,[9] who are viewed in terms of the ways they relate to the war for independence in which the whole of Algeria is involved. If education was a means of emancipation for a minority of women, the war, Djebar makes clear, was an opportunity for the rich and the poor, the learned and the illiterate, to liberate themselves from social and political oppression. The novel charts the painful transition from a passionate quest for personal identity, in which the seeker is opposed to society in general, to the arduous quest for national identity, in which the seeker is opposed not only to the restrictive world of the family but to the enslaving power of colonialism. It depicts the experiences a group of women undergo, as they become transformed, or transform themselves, from mothers, wives, and daughters into fully independent individuals who have to decide for themselves how they stand with regard to political action. It conveys a panoramic view of the revolution as it is witnessed by a variety of women – whether it is Lila who learns to come to terms with her pain and depression brought about by the death of her six-month-old baby and to reach out to other people; or Chérifa who, protected under her *haik*,[10] commits 'the great offence' of crossing the city alone to warn her husband that the authorities know of his involvement with the army of liberation; or Salima who resists interrogation and torture for a period of two weeks to emerge a defiant and courageous woman; or Hasiba who, at sixteen, is determined to take an active role in the revolution. What is clear is that, while each of them takes a different position and approach, all contribute to the creation of a new world. To borrow Evelyn Accad's comment, 'Assia Djebar's early novels reflect a progression in her ideas from an insistence upon the necessity of self-preoccupation in a world hostile to women to a recognition of the importance of awareness of others, to the resolution of personal problems through immersion in a national cause.'[11] In other words, nationalist and feminist causes are viewed as inseparable, and both are discussed equally critically as Djebar continues to write.

The author has said of the novels of her youth, *Romans de ma jeunesse*, that she produced them at great speed, each taking three to four months to write. Of the fourth novel, however, Djebar notes, 'I wrote it over a longer period, from 1962 to 1965: the first years of independence, in Algiers, where I used to do nothing but walk the streets. Nevertheless, once published, this novel led me into ten years of silence.'[12] What is it about *Les Allouettes naives*[13] that silenced her for so long?

The novel is set in Tunisia during the last months of the war of independence. However, instead of physical suffering and death, it portrays the romantic relationship of N'fissa and Rachid during their honeymoon. N'fissa is described as an emancipated woman who, nevertheless, remains attached to the values of traditional society. Following the pattern well established by now in the work of Assia Djebar, the novel explores the problems of this newly married couple as well as their sexual intimacy, which is an essential part of their quest to discover each other. The woman is no longer a passive body that submits to her husband in an act that resembles rape under cover of darkness, as described in *Les Enfants du nouveau monde*. She is now a partner who shares in the physical act of love and delights in the pleasures of her body. The novel also points to men's need to understand how they relate to their partners, for this is how the new woman and the new man of tomorrow will gain equality once the war is over. It looks at relationships between men and their prostitute mistresses, who are given an active role and a voice in the novel.[14] Notably it shows Rachid, the central character, moving freely between his family home and the brothel, and without distinguishing between wife and mistresses according to 'what traditions and myths have labelled good and bad, saintly and evil'.[15]

According to Djebar, the novel is polyphonic in its structure. It is also a record of her own experiences in Tunisia during the war of independence, and at the same time of many of the stories she heard from people in the refugee camp there. In an interview, she remarks:

> I wrote this novel between the ages of 27 and 30, soon after the independence of Algeria ... The main character is a masculine subject (*Je* / I). I wanted to create a chronicle of the Algerian youth of the years 1954 and 1962, in the masculine and in the feminine. ... It may be that the war between the people has ended, but another war is going to begin: a war between the sexes, between couples, or an inner war between the contradictions contained in every person. This, I feel, will not be easy.[16]

With *Les Allouettes naïves*, Assia Djebar found the major theme for the works that were to follow, and also undertook a number of new stylistic experiments. Yet publishing the novel was clearly a time of crisis for Djebar, both as a person and a writer. In her most recent book, *Ces Voix qui m'assiègent*, she explains the silence which lasted a decade. Of the 350 pages in the book, fifty were autobiographical. Once the novel was available to the public, she felt as if she wanted to cover her life and her own *self* with an immense veil: 'For a woman, if she cannot confine herself to fiction, writing subsequently becomes an act of disclosure, *dévoilement*.'[17] As an author she had succeeded in keeping her personal life distinct from her writing in her first three novels. With *Les Allouettes naïves*, she felt disturbed and threatened by her daring act of 'disclosure'. This goes to suggest that, unlike her heroines, Djebar had not entirely thrown off the yoke of restrictive customs that impose modesty on women, and found herself stranded between her ideal of a liberated woman and her sense of her actual self as someone still tied to convention. Her endless wanderings in the streets of Algiers in the years when she was working on the novel may be taken to signify her mental quest for the true meaning of freedom, both for the nation and for women.

From 1967 onwards, Djebar travelled extensively across Algeria, getting to know for the first time many areas of this vast country, and coming into contact with its people, particularly those who are never heard, who are denied a voice, and whose very existence is therefore denied. A question she asked herself was whether she had really succeeded in giving her female compatriots a voice, as she had hoped to do at the beginning of her career. She realized that writing in French had alienated her from the country's Arab women, the majority of whom are illiterate. In fact, even writing in classical Arabic would not have been much different, as these women only understand the colloquial Arabic spoken in Algeria. In order to come to terms with this dilemma and reconcile it with her own search for identity, Djebar decided to turn to film. She brought her decade of silence to an end in 1978 with *La Nouba des femmes du Mont Chenoua*,[18] her first film.

At the same time, her search for her '*self*' took her back to her mother's village high up in the mountains, where she came into close contact with women of her mother's and grandmother's generations, listening carefully to their conversations and talking with them in colloquial Algerian Arabic. The language became for Djebar the umbilical cord between herself, a French-educated woman, and these illiterate women, most of whom had never ventured beyond the boundaries of their village. Half-documentary and half-fiction, *La Nouba des femmes du Mont Chenoua* does not only give voice to women who lived through the shattering events of the war of independence, it also records their gestures and their postures as they tell their stories. Djebar's work is an attempt to preserve these voices, as well as to make them heard in the wider world.[19] The women's testimonies represent a female version of modern Algerian history, as distinct from the male version that has received official sanction.

Even so, the achievement is a limited one. Within an independent Algeria that is in many ways unfavourable to women, the film seems to confine them to their established role as guardians of tradition and custom, and fails to offer insights into the present, let alone the future. *La Nouba des femmes du Mont Chenoua* was criticized for its lack of a feminist vision: 'The production marks no progress on the issue of women's liberation. It dwells on the past and does not give a hearing to the young, who might have concerns that go beyond the transmission of their country's glorious history.'[20] While Djebar's exploration of her patrimony was an enriching experience that gave her images and dialogues that were to provide material for much of the fiction she wrote subsequently, she needed to set foot on more familiar and solid ground before she could venture out into the open spaces. In *Femmes d'Alger dans leur appartement*,[21] a collection of short stories written between 1958 and 1978 and published in 1980, she turned once again to urban Algeria and entered the closed homes inhabited by the secluded women of Algiers to paint a vivid picture of these forbidden, forgotten dwellings. The stories are written as if they were told to her by the women themselves and were translated directly from popular Arabic or, as Djebar put it, from 'a feminine Arabic: that of the underground ... a language that has withered away with never seeing the sun ... words of a veiled body, a language that has itself worn the veil for so long.'[22]

Set in two different time sequences, *Aujourd'hui* 'today' and *Hier* 'yesterday', the stories depict women from both the colonial and post-independence periods. The question they address is: has the revolution fulfilled its promises of justice and equality between the sexes? The evidence speaks for itself. The atmosphere of the whole volume is one of oppression, and the women speak in whispers. The stories cast light on the many violent acts to which Arab women submit, for example, the virginity that is brutally raped on the wedding night, and the silence imposed on women from girlhood when they are forced to lower their voice and gaze. To write about this subject becomes an act of transgression on the part of Assia Djebar. In a book which calls for solidarity among Arab women, she urges those who have achieved freedom of movement in body and spirit to think of those women of various age groups whose bodies remain prisoners of the veil but whose souls are in ferment as never before.

Femmes d'Alger dans leur appartement marks a definite break with Djebar's earlier works in many respects. Firstly, the depiction of couples, which had been prominent throughout her first four novels, is now completely abandoned and replaced with a call for female solidarity and sisterhood that will enable Arab women to face the atrocities of the present. Secondly, following the concern with personal/gender identity in her first two novels, which shifted to the search for national identity in her third and fourth novels, Djebar now turns to the wider sphere of the lives led by Arab–Muslim women in general, often rendered through resorting to female memory. All of these women share the common experience of the veil as a symbol of suppression as well as physical and psychological confinement to closed spaces. Djebar's perspective has grown more openly feminist, though not in a doctrinaire or theoretical fashion. Thirdly, as far as style is concerned, Djebar finally breaks with realism, the narrative drive and psychology of classic fiction. She uses other narrative modes and strategies in *Femmes d'Alger*, 'mixing historical chronicle, autobiography and real or invented lives'.[23] Finally, there is a general maturity of approach in *Femmes d'Alger dans leur appartement*, following which the author embarked on an ambitious literary project, the *Algerian Quartet*.

Djebar published *L'Amour, la fantasia*, translated as *Fantazia: An Algerian Cavalcade*,[24] the first volume of the *Algerian Quartet* in 1985. The novel is composed of two narratives: the first being an autobiographical journey undertaken by the author, the second being the history of Algeria during two particularly dramatic periods – the conquest of Algiers in 1830 and the war of liberation in 1954. Both narratives are related from a female point of view: the first focuses on the author's childhood as one of the first girls able to go to school during the colonial period, while the second tells the history of warfare as experienced by her female compatriots. Djebar uses oral records covering the post-1954 period which she gathered during the production of *La Nouba des femmes du Mont Chenoua*, and official French documents and French correspondence of the colonial period for the episodes from nineteenth-century history. The result is the creation of a novel described by its translator Dorothy Blair as 'an historical pageant, a dialectic between written (French) and oral (Arabic) personal accounts, an inquiry into the nature of the Algerian identity, and a personal quest'.[25] In other words, gender identity and national identity become a unified entity, which the author explores, not only through the pages of official history but also through women's oral testimonies, and Djebar's attempt at redefining the nation leads to a unique feminist perspective.

The novel opens with a little Arab girl being taken to school for the first time, 'one autumn morning, walking hand in hand with her father. A tall erect figure in a fez and a European suit, carrying a bag of school books' (*Fantazia*, p. 3). The father, a teacher in a French school, sets his daughter on a bilingual, bicultural, and highly contradictory journey by setting her free from the closed interiors of her mother's generation and, most importantly, by introducing her to the French language, a liberating yet simultaneously alienating instrument. Each of the three parts of the novel is based on a binary structure as Djebar alternates biographical scenes with historical episode. Memories of the narrator's early days at school give way to events relating to the French conquest in 1830. This alternation between the history of colonization and biographical scenes runs through the first two parts of the novel. In the third part, entitled 'Voice', written history is replaced by the oral testimony of the rural women interviewed by the author, giving their own version of the Algerian war. This leads to a deliberate differentiation of styles. While the episodes from 19th-century history are written in a very colourful manner, the oral accounts are transcribed into French without editing in a way that embeds Arabic idioms into a French language text. The technique results in 'an important element in the antiphonal structure of the work: dialogue between recent and more distant past; between personal and national experience; between writing and orality'.[26]

In addition to a narrative of girlhood memories and love stories, *Fantazia: An Algerian Cavalcade* contains highly visual scenes of violence, stories of death, rape, and bloodshed. It tells of the rape of Algeria by French imperialists, which she describes in terms of the destiny of a woman, and sometimes in terms of her own destiny. She identifies herself with a country that was reborn in 1842, though she was actually born in 1936, 'The date of my birth is *eighteen hundred and forty-two*, the year when General Saint-Arnaud arrives to burn down the *zaouia* of the Beni Menacer, the tribe from which I am descended.' (*Fantazia*, p. 217) The novel also deals with the violence of the war of liberation as witnessed by courageous women fighters who went into the battle zone. 'As a result of their courageousness, however, they found they had no place in a post-war society which preferred to repress the memory of their participation rather than face the difficult task of integrating this new type of woman into the social fabric.'[27] The disillusionment that dominates this novel indicates that the wounds left by the war of liberation are far from healed. Djebar predicts that there will be more violence and bloodshed. Moreover, as long as half of Algerian society is denied freedom, the 1954 revolution will have failed.

The second volume of the *Algerian Quartet, Ombre Sultane*, translated as *A Sister to Scheherazade*,[28] voices similar concerns but adds a call for female solidarity in the face of misogynous society. To Djebar, the situation of Arab-Muslim women has not changed fundamentally. On the contrary, women are becoming vulnerable to the regressive movements spreading throughout the Islamic world. Asked about the objective of *A Sister to Scheherazade*, Djebar replied, 'I posed the question: What does it mean, in a Muslim country, to have four wives?'[29] The novel challenges the reimposition of patriarchal values that restrict the position of women. More significantly, it reaffirms the principle of solidarity among women, a principle that is just as vital in the 1990s as ever, in view of the extremism of the Islamic fundamentalists, who use and abuse Islam for their own political aims, and declare their hatred of women whom they see as the source of all ills.

Alarmed by the misogynist claims disseminated at a threatening speed through populist discourse, Djebar interrupted her work on the *Algerian Quartet* and wrote *Loin de Médine, Filles d'Ismael*, translated as *Far From Madina*,[30] as a reply to the claims of the Islamic fundamentalists that women had no right to write history. A historian herself, she felt threatened as well as discredited; and in *Far From Madina*, a collection of stories which she prefers to call a novel, sets out to defy the fundamentalists in a double sense. First, going back to the texts of Ibn Hisham, Ibn Sa'ad, and al-Tabari, three historians who worked during the first two or three centuries of Islam, she rewrites the history of Islam as a woman and from a feminist perspective. Second, focusing on the active role played by women in early Islamic society, she recalls a key aspect of early Islam often neglected in historical works. The novel gives space to a variety of women – members of the Prophet's immediate family, migrant women, women from Medina and Mecca, rebel women, and Muslim women involved in fighting the enemies of the Prophet. It reminds religious extremists of women like Aisha, the Prophet's favourite wife, who was a respected and trusted authority on the Prophet's life and sayings; and the Prophet's daughter, Fatima, presenting her as the first woman to be betrayed in Islamic history when, following her father's death, she and her sisters in Islam were stripped of their rights. Djebar remarks:

> I was particularly struck by the fate of many women living during the period touched on in these pages, which begins with the death of Muhammad; I have tried to make them live again ...
> Muslims or non-Muslims ... they make their brief appearance, but in unforgettable circumstances, in the pages of chroniclers who were writing a century and a half, two centuries after the events; chroniclers, admittedly conscientious in recording the facts, but of course already habitually inclined to let any female presence be overshadowed.[31]

Far From Madina marks the author's movement away from the boundaries of the Algerian nation to the wider sphere of the 'Islamic nation'. It also marks the widening of her feminist concerns to include, besides the women of Algeria, other women of Islam, as Islamic fundamentalism gains a wider, international dimension. The brutality of the Islamic fundamentalists, it seems to Djebar, has surpassed anything that could have been imagined. From populist propaganda in the 1980s, they turned to ruthless terrorism and acts of barbaric violence in the 1990s. Islamic fundamentalists declared intellectuals and feminists as being among their main targets, and many of Djebar's friends were assassinated. Deeply hurt, she wrote the third volume of the *Algerian Quartet* as an expression of her great sense of loss.

Vaste est la prison, translated as *So Vast the Prison*,[32] follows the pattern established in the first two volumes and is made up of a mixture of private and public experience, history, and autobiography. The link between writing and history is here examined more intensively, and the autobiographical aspects are pursued with less circumspection. The narrative tells of the large number of Arab women whose lives have been turned into endless wanderings; and of the struggle of Algerian women for empowerment in defiance of the ethics of a patriarchal society. One interesting feature is the changing role of mothers and grandmothers who, ceasing to be guardians of the cultural heritage and its values, incite their daughters to escape from the *vast prison* of a stifling tradition, to break free, and breathe fresher air. However, the escalation of violence in Algeria stains the walls of their prison with more blood and plunges them into more violence, which makes Djebar wonder whether her writing itself has not always been marked by blood: 'By dint of writing about the dead of my inflamed land, last century, I thought that the blood of today's men (the blood of History and the oppression of women) arose to stain my writing, and to condemn me to silence.'[33] The atmosphere of the novel is, indeed, one of mourning and grief, but mourning is not enough. Djebar wants to know the reasons for this violence. In order to identify them, she embarks on an analysis of her country's history from the days of the Amazigh to the present, evoking the numerous colonialists that have invaded North Africa: the Romans, Arabs, Turks, and French. With the temporal scope of the narrative so broadened, writing is incontestably a public act rather than an exclusively aesthetic activity. The novel ends with a verse in which sorrow mingles with courage:

> Fugitive and knowing it in the middle of the race
> To write in order to ring the untiring pursuit
> The open circle closes at every pace
> Death ahead, encircled antelope
> Algeria the hunter, in, me is swallowed.[34]

These lines constitute the bridge between *Vaste est la prison* and *Le Blanc de l'Algérie*,[35] written in close succession and characterized by the same tone of voice. Lacerated with the pain of losing her loved ones in the midst of a horrifying fratricidal war, Djebar wrote *Le Blanc de l'Algérie* as a reaction to the tragic moments she shared with her compatriots, and dedicated it to three close friends – Mahfoud Boucebci, M'Hamed Boukhobza, and Abelkader Alloula – who were all savagely assassinated by Islamic terrorists. '[The novel] corresponds to the necessity to remember, to testify, and to pay homage to the victims of the blind war.'[36] The end of the war for independence did not bring an end to bloodshed and, ironically, the symbol of Algerian independence is not *the white of peace* but the colours of violence. The roots of this violence were not severed with the end of colonial rule but continues to be fed by the rulers of Algeria after independence. According to Djebar, barbarism cannot be attributed merely to the work of the fundamentalists, nor are the assassins always the fundamentalists. Rather, the ruling elite must bear much of the responsibility:

> Here comes the time of the assassins! It's coming? No, alas, this bloody era was already there, had slid in among us, in the midst of yesterday's war, and we did not know it. We learned of it only after 1962, and then only from snatches of vague confessions, of half-suggested confessions.[37]

Le Blanc de l'Algérie is a most powerful work in which Djebar digs out the buried truth. Fearless of the consequences, she utters that which is usually left unsaid about the government of Algeria and the country's heroes, whose hands are often anything but clean. The white of Algeria can be said to be the colour of the shroud that *some* of her enemies have prepared for her. Djebar speaks for her beloved Algeria and cries with all her might for its rescue. *Le Blanc de l'Algérie* is therefore dominated by an urgency of tone, but, as Djebar remarks:

> Every voice of urgency gets chipped away before it can even find itself, as the trembling light of its own quest. ...Yet I am driven only by this particular necessity of a voice in view of the imminence of disaster.
> Writing and its urgency.
> Writing to express the Algeria which sways and for which some are preparing the white shroud.[38]

Stylistically powerful and rich in content, *Le Blanc de l'Algérie* will retain a special place in the work of Djebar. The mere fact that she challenges the violence going on in the world by writing of violence is ample proof of her commitment to justice, and her determination to oppose the forces of backwardness in both colonial and post-independence

Algeria.

For Assia Djebar, writing is a form of direct action, of bearing witness, of commitment, and transgression. Above all, her writing is intended to give voice to those who are forgotten by official forms of discourse, the marginalized, betrayed, and forgotten women of Islam, whom it urges to advance with defiance, anger, and hope.

NOTES

1. Assia Djebar, *Ces Voix qui m'assiégent* (Paris: Albin Michelle, 1999), pp. 25-27. Quotations from the following works by Assia Djebar have been translated into English by the present author: *La Soif, Les Impatients, Les Enfants du nouveau monde, Les Allouettes naives, Femmes d'Alger dans leurs appartement, Vaste est la prison, Le Blanc de l'Algérie,* and *Ces Voix qui m'assiégent.*
2. See Valérie Budig-Markin, 'Writing and Filming the Cries of Silence', *World Literature Today,* Autumn (1996), p. 893: 'Writing gives voice and form to the silences / signs of the temporal and spatial infinity which gives meaning to life.'
3. Assia Djebar, *La Soif* (Paris: Julliard, 1957). All further references are to this edition and are included in the text.
4. Zahia Smail Salhi, *Politics, Poetics and the Algerian Novel* (Lewiston, N.Y.: Edwin Mellen Press, 1999), p. 202. FLN stands for Front de Libération Nationale (National Liberation Front).
5. Djebar, *Ces Voix qui m'assiégent,* p. 18.
6. Abdelkabir Khatibi, *Le Roman Maghrébin* (Paris: Maspéro, 1968), p. 62. Translated into English by the present author.
7. Assia Djebar, *Les Impatients* (Paris: Jullard, 1958).
8. See Smail Salhi, *Politics, Poetics and the Algerian Novel,* p. 198.
9. Assia Djebar, *Les Enfants du nouveau monde* (Paris: Julliard, 1962). Djebar includes a list of twenty characters at the opening of the novel as a guide.
10. *Haik,* a white veil mostly worn in North Africa.
11. Evelyn Accad, 'Assia Djebar's Contribution to Arab Women's Literature: Rebellion, Maturity, Vision', *World Literature Today,* Autumn 1996, p. 807.
12. Djebar, *Ces Voix qui m'assiégent,* p. 64.
13. Assia Djebar, *Les Allouettes naives* (Paris: Julliard, 1967).
14. The title, *Les Allouettes naives,* translated as *The Naive Larks,* refers to the name given by the French legionnaires to the prostitute dancers of the Ouled Nail tribe of southern Algeria.
15. Evelyn Accad and R. Ghurayyib, *Contemporary Arab Women Writers and Poets* (Beirut: Beirut University College, 1985), pp. 25-26.
16. Kamal Salhi, 'Assia Djebar Speaking: An Interview with Assia Djebar', *International Journal of Francophone Studies,* 2:3 (1999) 168-79.
17. Djebar, *Ces Voix qui m'assiégent,* p. 64.
18. Nouba: Algerian military band, meaning here the battle of women from Mount Chenoua. The film was awarded the Critics' Prize at the Venice Biennale in 1979. A second film-documentary *La Zerda et les chants de l'oubli,* 1982, explores historical aspects of the Maghreb during the French protectorate in Morocco.
19. For a more detailed study of this film see Zahia Smail Salhi, 'Maghrebi Women Film-makers and the Challenge of Modernity: Breaking Women's Silence', in *Women and the Media in the Arab World,* ed., Naomi Sakr (London: I B Tauris, 2004).

20. J.P. Monego, *Maghrebian Literature in French*, p. 139.
21. Assia Djebar, *Femmes d'Alger dans leur appartement* (Paris: Des femmes, 1980). The title was inspired by Delacroix's painting of the same name. In her postscript to the book, Djebar states that in 1832, in the newly conquered city of Algiers, Delacroix visited a harem for a few hours. He left with a masterpiece *Femmes d'Alger dans leur appartement* which remains *a stolen glimpse.*
22. Djebar, *Femmes d'Alger dans leur appartement*, pp. 7–8.
23. David Coward, 'Assia Djebar: an Overview', in *Francophone Voices*, ed., Kamal Salhi (Exeter: Elm Bank Publications, 1999), p. 60.
24. Assia Djebar, *L'Amour, la fantasia* (Paris: J.-C. Lattes, 1985). For this novel I have used the version *Fantazia: An Algerian Cavalcade*, trans. Dorothy S. Blair (London: Quartet Books, 1985). All further references are to this translation (*Fantazia*) and included in the text.
25. Dorothy Blair, 'Introduction', *Fantazia: An Algerian Cavalcade*, np.
26. Blair, 'Introduction', *Fantazia: An Algerian Cavalcade*, np.
27. Katherine Graki, 'Writing Violence and the Violence of Writing in Assia Djebar's *Algerian Quartet*', *World Literature Today*, Autumn 1996, pp. 835-43.
28. Assia Djebar, *Ombre Sultane* (Paris: J.-C. Lattes, 1987). Here too I have used the version *A Sister to Scheherazade*, trans. Dorothy S. Blair (London: Quartet Books, 1987).
29. Mildred P. Mortimer, 'Entretien avec Assia Djebar, écrivain algérien', *Research in African Literatures*, 2:19 (1988) 205.
30. Assia Djebar, *Loin de Médine, Filles d'Ismael* (Paris: Albin Michelle, 1991). I have used the version *Far From Madina*, trans. Dorothy S. Blair (London: Quartet Books, 1994).
31. Djebar, *Far from Medina*, 1994, p. xv.
32. Assia Djebar, *Vaste est la prison* (Paris: Albin Michelle, 1995); for a translated version, see *So Vast a Prison*, trans. Betsy Wing (New York: Seven Stories, 1999).
33. Djebar, *Vaste est la prison*, p. 337
34. Djebar, *Vaste est la prison*, p. 348. Translation by Hafid Gafaiti.
35. Assia Djebar, *Le Blanc de l'Algérie* (Paris: Albin Michel, 1995).
36. Hafid Gafaiti, 'The Blood of Writing: Assia Djebar's Unveiling of Women and History', *World Literature Today*, Autumn 1996, p. 818.
37. Djebar, *Le Blanc de l'Algérie*, p. 232.
38. Djebar, *Le Blanc de l'Algérie*, p. 272.

PADMINI MONGIA

New Delhi, Atrani

April in New Delhi, bougainvillea
white, pink, rose, and purple,
suddenly it's early summer in Atrani,
the crimson wall receding
behind the heaving boat.

The Moorish dome of the church –
mosaic of yellow and blue tiles –
shrinks into the shimmering sky. At *La Tonnarella*
we drape ourselves on hot rocks,
awaiting grilled anchovies, that morning's catch.

Yachts drift from Naples and Capri.
We scorn their wealthy patrons,
willing them to other shores.
All around is frilled blue water,
above are sheer rocks and stone steps.

One evening, a storm returns with us.
The boat crashes down to the slap
of each wave. You steer the boat,
I clutch its sides, straining for a glimpse
of flowers, for a blue and yellow dome.

When they pull the boat in, they tell us
we should have known how to read the signs.
A decade later, in New Delhi,
I know they were right. We should have known
how to read crimson.

Atrani is a small town on the Amalfi coast.

Vaishnu Devi

(for Shashi Agrawal)

At first, it was a game. I led from hill to hill:
I hid behind the flame of the forest,

threw its thick red flowers on the stony path.
Bhairon picked up the flowers and followed.

I parted the hair of bushes to reveal scented buds.
Bhairon breathed them in, pushed back the hair.

He stayed one step behind. I felt his breath,
but his warm skin never grazed mine.

Before I could lead him to the secret stream,
he changed. He crushed the flowers,

threw his large legs from red stone to red stone,
made me pant into the slit where water flowed,

and rocks drew blood. Still he chased
and still I ran till I reached Bhawan, home,

where stones were my bed and water my covers.
Outside the cave, Bhairon sat and wept.

'No pilgrimage to me will be complete
without one to you,' I granted, so he'd stop sobbing.

Centuries have passed, and they continue to come,
Hindus, Christians, Sikhs, even Muslims.

Slippers on his hands, leg stumps
in the air, the leper walks up from Katra to Bhawan.

From Jammu young men come,
climbing the long road in repeated prostration.

In a *palki*, an old woman is hoisted. Children are cajoled,
small horses are whipped, streaming pilgrims

chant to me for strength, imitating my journey,
my slow escape from the demon.

Centuries have passed. I am the virgin mother,
the goddess astride a tiger, the smoothed stones of caves,

the gentle trickle of water. I am the force within,
I am the strength without. I guide the cripple up the hill,

the pony down the rocks. Yet I regret
that I am half-virgin, half-married, *Adh Kuwari*,

forever tainted by Bhairon's desire. It's true I teased,
but I only wanted to play the mountain goat, to ripple with the stream.

I have heard of others, of one who became a tree
even as the sun-god grasped her thigh.

Did I wait too long? Should I never have strewn the flowers?
Or should I have followed him up another mountain

to the cave surrounded by pomegranates, where he lived.

Almost True

I embrace all passing gods:
genuflect to Christ, fold hands
for Krishna, Ganesh, and Shiv.
In calm, approach the Buddha
and chant the Koran when I can.

Poetry I chant too and embrace
the bright morning, the polished stone,
the bare tree or the wide river.
I kiss the child's arm, the baby's foot.
I rumple curly heads: all gods, all wonder.

Breaking the Mirror of Urdu Verse: Speech and Silence in the Poetry of Kishwar Naheed

AMINA YAQIN

Kishwar Naheed has written and recited poetry for more than thirty years, edited newspapers and magazines, and worked for the Pakistani civil service for the same length of time. It is ironic that official censoring of her literary career triggered by her job as a civil servant has afforded her greater public visibility and lent an added urgency to her writings. She has assumed the persona of an activist, a poet, a historian and a chronicler in Urdu. Not content with her work as a feminist activist she has edited a volume of feminist essays in English and facilitated translations of her own poetry into English.[1]

Naheed was born in 1940 in Bulandshahr, a township of Uttar Pradesh in India. In September 1949, two years after Partition, her family migrated to West Pakistan and settled in Lahore. At nine years of age, this change spelt the end of her Indian primary schooling and led to a new education and beginning. Her love of Urdu poetry began at home where she was exposed to the oral tradition and literary heritage from an early age. The hazy childhood memory of a *mushaira* held at her parent's home is one of her foremost associations with Urdu poetry. She herself began writing poetry towards the last stages of her secondary education and she participated in a public *mushaira* for the first time after joining Government College. Her subsequent development as a literary figure is directly linked to her voracious appetite for reading, writing, and translating poetry.

Naheed enrolled at Government College when she was nineteen years old. A year later she married the Urdu poet Yousaf Kamran, and at twenty-two was the mother of two children. She was disowned by her family for marrying outside the Sayyid clan and, separated from her parental home, Naheed temporarily abandoned her higher education in order to make ends meet in her conjugal home. She was able to successfully complete her Masters in Economics in 1961. However, surrounded by hostile in-laws, and by poets and critics who were mostly her husband's cronies, she felt isolated in her new environment. Her identity as a poet was changed by her marriage, particularly as she found her independent pursuit of poetry trivialized by critics as a subsidiary undertaking compared to her husband's 'real job' as a poet. Increasingly marginalized, she transferred this personal experience into a major theme in her poetry.[2]

During the 1960s, in spite of familial constraints, she became a well-known public voice on the airwaves as a regular presenter on Radio Pakistan programmes, and, in 1966, she started appearing in Lahore television programmes. Her interest in the media is also reflected in the research she undertook for the national archives, while she was in post as the Director General of the National Council of Arts in Islamabad. During her period in office, she compiled databases on the visual and performing arts, productions of reprints from fine art, and collections of folk, classical, and semi-classical music in Pakistan.

As a journalist, she held editorial positions at the Urdu political weekly *Pak Jamhuriat* and the monthly *Mah-e nau* from 1977 to 1980 and from 1984 to 1988. In 1981 she edited the Urdu literary journal, *Adab-e latif*.[3] Her formative years in Pakistan were spent under the military regimes of Ayub Khan and Yahya Khan. In September 1971, she was sent on an official visit to East Pakistan to write a booklet promoting the image of the army officials even though they were committing atrocities against Bengali civilians. What she saw deeply affected her and the report she submitted was censored and discarded. She and other supporters of East Pakistan were labelled as unpatriotic and as traitors. An outspoken intellectual, Kishwar Naheed attracted the attention of the Central Intelligence Unit from 1977 to 1979. She particularly remembers the atmosphere of oppression and intolerance during the martial law regimes of Ayub Khan (1958-1969), Yahya Khan (1969-1971), and of Zia-ul-Haq (1977-1988). Her husband and his father were both jailed in 1970 for speaking out against martial law and ridiculing army officers. To Naheed, the memory of Yousaf Kamran's year in imprisonment is a bitter reminder of that time.[4]

Naheed has represented Pakistan at international women's conferences. Her first conference paper, on Pakistani women's literature, was presented in Iran in 1971. She gradually moved out of the national arena into the international with her participation in the Afro-Asian Writers Conference in 1973; the Berlin Congress of World Women in 1975; the Egypt National Conference of Muslim women in 1976; and the gathering of Muslim women leaders and professionals in Manila in 1981. During the 1980s she also consolidated her writing skills, attending creative writing workshops in India, the Philippines, Canada, and the United States. The years following saw her time evenly divided between literary pursuits and performative feminist activity.[5]

During the 1990s, Naheed devoted a good deal of her energies to official duties in her capacity as Director General of the National Council of Arts in Islamabad. While working for the government, she also set up her own non-government organization, Hawwa Associates, which works toward securing better contracts for home-based piece-rate female workers from rural areas. She says she finally stepped down from the Arts Council directorship in 1999, as she was tired of the instability of her job, brought about by changing regimes and their interference with the civil service.[6]

The selection of poems below has been taken from different volumes of Naheed's poetry and offer an introductory sampling of her work. The first poem 'Kare kos' ('A distance of two miles') has been chosen from *Benam masafat (Anonymous journey)*, her second collection of poetry spanning the years 1969-1971.[7] This poem reflects a conflict between speech and silence, and its theme is representative of Naheed's work. It is also significant that Naheed traverses the 'distance of two miles' in free verse instead of the stylized ghazal. Her alienation as a woman poet within the traditionally male world of Urdu poetry can, it seems, only be expressed in a modern form which allows her to create her own metaphors and meaning.

The next two poems 'Censorship' and 'Mom mahal' ('Wax palace'), both written in the early 1980s, have been selected from the collection entitled *Siyah hashiye men gulabi rang (Pink hue in a black margin)*.[8] 'Censorship' draws attention to the hegemonic forces of the authoritarian regime of General Zia-ul-Haq, which tried to legitimize its own reality for the people of Pakistan, while 'Mom mahal' is a symbolic poem expressing the powerlessness of women's lives in low income households and the pathos of a mother-daughter relationship. These poems are followed by a selection of verse written in the latter half of the 1980s and the early 1990s and published in *Khiyali shakhs se muqabala (Contending with an imaginary person)*.[9] 'Apahaj ma mitti ki goldan jublee' ('The golden jubilee of a crippled motherland') is a pre-emptive work, speculating bleakly on the fiftieth anniversary of Pakistan's independence which would take place in 1997. In contrast is 'Apni jaisi aurat vazir-e azam se muqalima' ('Dialogue with a woman Prime Minister like myself'), a poem echoing nationalist concerns at the end of military rule in 1988 and pondering upon the beginning of a new era under Benazir Bhutto. The last poem 'Taliban se qibla ru guftugu' ('A casual conversation with the Taliban') is from her compilation entitled *Main pehle janam men rat thi* (*I was night in my first incarnation*), published in 1998.[10] This poem underlines the return of an intolerant sensibility toward women in Pakistan amid the growing popularity of the political group, the Taliban.

A distance of two miles (*Kare kos*) کڑے کوس

When a letter of the alphabet	حرف ،
Became imprisoned in the shackles of speech	گویائی کی زنجیر میں جب قید ہوا
It became a noun	اسم بنا
It became a covenant	عہد بنا
It became a poem	نظم بنا
It became a sorrowful quest in the story of labour and sweat	قصۂ کام و دہن کا غم مطلوب بنا
It became outstanding and mediocre	خوب و ناخوب بنا
The unsaid letter of the alphabet	حرفِ ناگفتہ
Became but an affliction of the mind	مگر ذہن کا آزار بنا
It became a wall around the heart	دل کی دیوار بنا
It became an arduous path	راہ دشوار بنا ۔
It did not become the lost tale of an eternal love	قصۂ شوق کی وارفت کہانی نہ بنا
It did not become the afflicted token of a fraudulent union	حیلۂ وصل کی غم دیدہ نشانی نہ بنا ۔
The destination of speech is the gallows	دار ہے منزلِ گویائی
Everyone knows.	سبھی جانتے ہیں
That the wounds from the unspoken letter of the alphabet are mine	حرفِ ناگفتہ کے یہ زخم مگر میرے ہیں
Whom my loneliness	جن کو تنہائی مری ،
Besides myself knows.	مجھ سے سوا ، جانتی ہے

Censorship

In those days when the camera
    could not freeze frame injustice
You should have written the history of oppression
    and given it the name of courage
Up to those times.

Today, through the images
    captured on celluloid, we can imagine
What the depiction would have been
    of the accompanying noise and vision of
Trees crumbling from their disintegrating roots
    on mountainous slopes
Whether you are happy or sorrowful
You still breathe
By blinking eyes open or shut
The outline and outlook of our minds does not change
The uprooted branch of a tree in the river
Remains wood
It does not transform into a crocodile
We have been standing for a long time on the rooftops of stories
Thinking that the city belongs to us
The walls of the foundation have sunk
But we are still perched on the rooftops of stories
Understanding life to be
Those substantial breaches in broken bricks
Strewn across the ruined alleys of colourless afternoons.

جن زمانوں میں کیمرہ ظلم کو ہمیشہ کے لئے
مجسم نہیں کر سکتا تھا
تمہیں ان زمانوں تک ہی
ظلم کو بہادری کا نام دینے کی تاریخ لکھنی چاہیے تھی۔
آج سلولائیڈ پہ منتقل منظروں کو دیکھ کر اندازہ ہوتا ہے
کہ پہاڑی ڈھلوانوں پہ جڑوں سے ٹوٹتے درختوں کی آواز اور
منظر نامہ کیسا ہوتا ہے ۔
چاہے تم خوش ہو یا افسردہ
سانس تو لیتے ہو۔
آنکھیں کھولنے یا بند کرنے سے
ذہن پہ نقش، منظر نہیں بدلتا ہے ،
دریا میں گرے درخت کا تنا
لکڑی کا ہی رہتا ہے
مگر مچھ نہیں بنتا ہے۔
ہم کب سے کہانیوں کی چھتوں پہ چڑھے
یہ سوچے ہے ہیں
کہ یہ شہر ہمارا ہے
بنیاد کی دیواروں کی زمین بیٹھ گئی ہے
مگر اب تک ہم کہانیوں کی چھتوں پہ چڑھے
پھیکی دوپہروں کی اجڑی گلیوں کی ٹوٹی اینٹوں کی
چوڑی دراڑوں کو زندگی سمجھے ہے ہیں

(Siyah hashiye)

Wax palace (*Mom mahal*)

موم محل

Before my marriage my Ma
Would get frightened in her dreams.
Her terrified screams would awaken me
I would stir her, asking what had happened
And with vacant eyes she would keep on staring.
She could not remember those dreams.
One night startled by her dream
She did not scream,
Fearfully she had held me tight
I asked her the story?
As she opened her eyes,
      she offered a prayer of thanks and said,
'In my dream I saw,
That you were drowning and I had
jumped into the river to save you'
And that night lightning struck
Electrocuting our buffalo and my fiancé.
One night Ma was sleeping and I was awake,
Ma kept clenching and unclenching
      her fist over and over,
And it seemed as if she was tiring
      from holding on to something,
Yet mustering up courage again she would
      clench her fist once more.
I roused Ma
But Ma did not tell me her dream.
Since that day I cannot sleep
I have come into the other courtyard,
Now both Ma and I scream in our dreams.
And when someone asks,
We say
We do not remember our dreams.

میرے بیاہ سے پہلے میری ماں
خواب میں ڈر جایا کرتی تھی
اُس کی خوفناک چیخوں سے میری آنکھ کُھل جاتی تھی
میں اُسے جگاتی، ماجرا پوچھتی
اور وہ خالی آنکھوں گھورتی رہتی
اُسے خواب یاد نہیں رہتے تھے۔
ایک رات خواب میں ڈر کر
اس نے چیخ نہیں ماری
خوف زدہ ہو کر مجھے اپنے ساتھ چپٹا لیا تھا
میں نے ماجرا پوچھا
تو اس نے آنکھیں کھول کر شکرانہ ادا کرتے ہوئے کہا،
"میں نے خواب میں دیکھا تھا
تم ڈوب رہی ہو اور میں نے تمہیں بچانے کو دریا میں چھلانگ لگائی ہے ۔ ۔"
اور اُس رات بجلی گرنے سے
ہماری بھینس اور میرا منگیتر جل گئے تھے ۔
ایک رات ماں سو رہی تھی اور میں جاگ رہی تھی،
ماں بار بار مٹھی بند کرتی اور کھولتی
اور یوں لگتا کہ جیسے کچھ پکڑنے کی کوشش میں تھک کر
مگر پھر ہمت باندھتے کو مٹھی بند کرتی ہے ۔
میں نے ماں کو جگایا
مگر ماں نے مجھے خواب بتانے سے انکار کر دیا ۔
اُس دن سے میری نیند اڑ گئی،
میں دوسرے صحن میں آگئی،
اب میں اور میری ماں دونوں خواب میں چیخیں مارتے ہیں
اور جب کوئی پوچھے
تو کہہ دیتے ہیں
ہمیں خواب یاد نہیں رہتے۔

(*Siyah hashiye*)[12]

The golden jubilee of a crippled motherland
(Apahaj ma mitti ki goldan jublee)

اپاہج ماں مٹی کی گولڈن جوبلی

Hear me!
I am addressing you
I am Pakistan!
Your motherland
I was born from the wombs of hope
Nurtured by those who are not amongst us anymore.

Those honest people
Who saw the dream of a separate nation.
A vision of such a land
In which they and their future generations
Could, with pride and freedom,
      be part of the human race.
Those sincere people
Who bartered with their lives
for the realisation of their dream
I am the outcome of that wish
Made by those true people

As I turned twenty-four
Whirlpools of dishonesty crippled me.

Now forty-three years old
I am frightened and unsafe

Hopes keep eluding me

I am not a forgotten lesson
I am not a broken branch
But what sort of smoke is this
That keeps clouding over the freedom
      in my eyes
What sparks are these
That continue to scorch
      the triumphs of my ancestors
What kind of fear is this?
That is transforming the gushing blood
      of my veins to an icy shame.
Swept along by the wind, I too

میری سنو !
میں تم سے مخاطب ہوں
میں پاکستان ہوں !
تمہاری ماں مٹی
میں نے ان لوگوں کی امیدوں کی
کوکھ سے جنم لیا تھا
جواب ہم تم میں نہیں ہیں ۔
وہ سچے لوگ
جنہوں نے ایک علیحدہ مملکت کا خواب دیکھا تھا
ایک ایسی مملکت کا خواب
کہ جس میں وہ اور ان کی آئندہ آنے والی نسلیں
آزادی اور فخر سے خود کو انسان کہہ سکیں
وہ سچے لوگ
جنہوں نے اس خواب کی تعبیر کے لیے
اپنی زندگیوں کا سودا کیا تھا ۔
میں ان ہی سچے لوگوں کے
خوابوں کی تعبیر ہوں ۔
میں چوبیس سال کی ہوئی
تو جھوٹ کے گماشتوں نے مجھے اپاہج کر دیا ۔
میں ۴۳ سال کی ہوکے بھی
خوفزدہ اور غیر محفوظ ہوں
امیدیں مجھ سے چھپتی پھر رہی ہیں
میں کوئی بھولا ہوا سبق نہیں ہوں
میں کوئی ٹوٹی ہوئی شاخ نہیں ہوں
مگر یہ کیسا دھواں ہے
جو میری آزادی کی آنکھوں کو دھندلانے چلے جا رہا ہے
یہ کون سے شعلے ہیں
جو میرے اسلاف کی فتح مندیوں کو جھلساتے دے رہے ہیں
یہ کیسا خوف ہے
جو میری رگوں میں جوش مار نے خون کو شرمساری کی
برف میں دھنستے دے رہا ہے
میں نے تو ہوا کے پروں پر بھی
"لے کے رہیں گے پاکستان" لکھا تھا

Wrote, 'we will have Pakistan'
The butterflies too in those days
Wore the colours of my flag

I had placed the oil burner of freedom
On my doorstep because
It would be a guiding light for enslaved nations
That wanted freedom

Who was it?
That took my reverberating slogans
And left behind poisonous machinations.

My children!
The children of my honourable people
By forgetting your heritage
How long will you cheat your conscience?
And wear false promises

My children!
I don't need your words
It is not your destiny to regain the history
Of a moth-eaten map or a torn picture.

Listen to my request!
Return the stature of my white hair to me
Return the peace of my womb to me
Rise my children! I am addressing you
Who else can a mother speak to!

(*Khiyali shakhs*)

Dialogue with a woman Prime Minister like myself
(*Apni jaisi aurat vazir-e azam se muqalima*)

I am the caretaker of this garden, mother
Give me some rights over the garden too, mother!

My arms are all blue with bruises
Needles have pricked my eyes
Wounds decorate my lips
My feet are covered in blisters

میرے زمانے میں تو تتلیوں نے بھی
میرے پرچم کا رنگ پہنا تھا
میں نے اپنی دہلیز پر آزادی کا دیا
اس لیے رکھا تھا
کہ غلام قوم اس کی روشنی میں
آزاد ہونا سیکھیں گی
وہ کون تھا
جو میرے گونجتے نعرے لے کر
زہرناک سرگوشیاں چھوڑ گیا ہے ۔
میرے بچّو !
میرے سچے لوگوں کے بچّو
تم اپنی وراثت کو بھول کر
کب تک اپنے ضمیر کو جھٹلا تے
اور جھوٹے وعدوں کو پہنتے رہو گے
میرے بچّو !
مجھے تمہارے لفظ نہیں چاہئیں
پھٹی ہوئی تصویر یا پھٹے ہوئے نقشے کی
تاریخ رقم کرنا ، تمھارا مقدر نہیں ہے ۔
میری نیّتی حُسنو !
مجھے میرے سفید بالوں کا وقار واپس لوٹا دو
مجھے میری کوکھ میں پلنے والا امن واپس لوٹا دو
اٹھو میرے بچّو ! میں تم سے مخاطب ہوں
ماں ! بھلا اور کس سے بات کر سکتی ہے !

اپنی جیسی عورت وزیر اعظم سے مکالمہ

میں باغ کی راکھی ہوئی میّا
مجھے باغ پہ حق بھی دو میّا
مرے بازو نیلو نیل ہیں سب
مری آنکھوں میں سوئیاں ہیں چبھی
مرے ہونٹوں پہ ہیں زخم سجے
مرے پاؤں میں چھالے ہیں بہت
میں کیسے پھولوں اے میّا
وہ کوڑے جو میری کمر پہ ہیں

How can I forget, o mother!
Those lashes imprinted upon my back
That imprisonment which overpowers my body
Sticking like a snake to its newborn

I remember all those decisions
Which came out on the behest of religion
Which cast a shadow upon my witness
Which were named as Shariat
Which were called truth and justice
Those wounds incurred, allegations made

O mother shall I remind you
That those hands are still living
Those hands which performed the stoning
On my tiny flowerlike children
Those hands which snatched the chadar
Assaulted and battered my sisters
They passed time easily
They sold each and every particle
They had no respect for even the earth

You must remember, o mother
How our homes turned into jails
How sparkling bodies faded
We were homeless in our homeland
We had been labelled worthless

You must remember, o mother
That raging hell, those ruined homes
They whose lives were taken by execution
Their blood was not less honourable
Their life was not without courage
Bearing witness from all of them
Enduring their sorrow

Shall I admonish you, o mother?
Do not forget that this is a loan to you
Do not forget that this is your obligation
I am the caretaker of this garden, mother
Give me some rights over the garden too, mother.

(Khiyali shakhs)

وہ تیر جو میرے وجود پہ
سانپ سنپولے بن بیٹھی
وہ سارے فیصلے یاد مجھے
جو نام پہ مذہب کے آئے
جو میری گواہی پہ چھائے
جو نام شریعت کا پائے
جو حق و صداقت کہلائے
جو زخم لگے، الزام آئے

تمہیں یاد دلاؤں اے میّا
وہ ہاتھ سلامت ہیں اب تک
جن ہاتھوں نے سنگسار کیے
مرے ننھے پھول سے بچوں کو
جن ہاتھوں نے چادر چھینی
مری بہنوں کو زد و کوب کیا
جو چاٹ گئے دیواریں بھی
جو بیچ گئے ذرہ ذرہ
جنہیں لاج نہ آئی مٹی کی

تمہیں یاد تو ہوگا اے میّا
کیا جیل بنے تھے گھر اپنے
کیا اُجلے تن دُھند لائے تھے
ہم اپنے دیس میں بے گھر تھے
ہم بے قیمت کہلائے تھے۔

تمہیں یاد تو ہوگا اے میّا
جو حشر اُٹھے جو گھر اُجڑے
جو مقتل میں جاں ہار گئے
خوں ان کا کم عظمت تو نہ تھا
جاں ان کی بے ہمّت تو نہ تھی
ان سب کی گواہی لے کے میں
ان سب کی دُہائی لے کے میں

یہ تم کو جتاؤں اے میّا
مت بھولنا تم پہ قرض ہے یہ
مت بھولنا تم پہ فرض ہے یہ
میں باغ کی راکھی رہوئی میّا
مجھے باغ پہ حق بھی دو میّا !

A casual conversation with the Taliban
(Taliban se qibla ru guftagu)

طالبان سے قبلہ رو گفتگو

They who became scared of little girls
They who are fugitives to knowledge
They speak of God Almighty
Who gave the command to seek knowledge
Yet they make proclamations beyond what is divine obligation

وہ جو بچوں سے بھی ڈر گئے
وہ جو علم سے بھی گریز پا
کریں ذکر رب کریم کا
وہ جو حکم دیتا ہے علم کا
کریں اس کے حکم سے ماورا
یہ منادیاں

No hand should grasp a book
No fingers should grip a pen
There should be no occasion to write a name
Nor a ceremony for a female naming

نہ کتاب ہو کسی ہاتھ میں
نہ ہی انگلیوں میں قلم رہے
کوئی نام لکھنے کی جا نہ ہو
نہ ہو رسمِ اسم زنان کوئی

They who became scared of little girls
They go from city to city making proclamations,
To cover up
Those shameful sexual female bodies

وہ جو بچوں سے بھی ڈر گئے
کریں شہر شہر منادیاں
کہ ہر ایک قدِ حیا نما کو
نقاب دو

And quell every question from those hearts
With this answer
We do not want
These girls
To soar above like winged birds
We do not want
That these girls
Should go to seminaries even, leave alone offices
Some are fiery sparks and some toe the line
At least there are some
Whose destination is the sacred courtyard in Mecca
This is the obligation
This is the word

کہ ہر ایک دل کے سوال کو
یہ جواب دو
نہیں چاہیے
کہ یہ لڑکیاں
اڑیں طائروں کی طرح بلند
نہیں چاہیے
کہ یہ لڑکیاں
کہیں مدرسوں، کہیں دفتروں کا بھی رخ کریں
کوئی شعلہ رو، کوئی باصفا
ہے کوئی تو صحنِ حرم ہی
اس کا مقام ہے۔
یہی حکم ہے
یہ کلام ہے

They who became scared of little girls
They are close, not far from here
See them, recognise them
There is not much expectation from them
In the fallen city
Keep your faith and uphold your belief
That they who became scared of little girls

وہ جو بچوں سے بھی ڈر گئے
وہ یہیں کہیں ہیں قریب میں
انہیں دیکھ لو، انہیں جان لو
نہیں ان سے کچھ بھی بعید
شہرِ زوال میں
رکھو حوصلہ، رکھو یہ یقین
کہ جو بچوں سے بھی ڈر گئے

Are very small in stature.   وہ ہیں کتنے چھوٹے وجود میں۔

Make proclamations in every city   کرو شہر شہر منادیاں

Keep your faith and uphold your belief   رکھو حوصلہ، رکھو یہ یقیں

That they who became scared of little girls   کہ جو بچیوں سے بھی ڈر گئے

Are very small in stature.   وہ ہی کتنے چھوٹے وجود ہیں۔

(*Pehle janam*)

A Note on the translations

I began working on the translations of Kishwar Naheed's poetry when I was researching my PhD thesis at SOAS.[13] At that time, a useful selection of her poetry was already available in English translation but it was not extensive. I was keen to include new translations of her poems in my thesis in order to broaden the scope of my analysis. Paradoxically the incentive to write my own versions grew with comparing different translations of the same poem and noting the variations among them. Two of the poems I initially worked on were 'Mom mahal' and 'Censorship', both of which had been translated before. I was drawn to 'Mom mahal' because of its representation of the false consciousness that permeates women's lives in Pakistan, the ambiguity of a mother-daughter relationship, and social constructions of gender. One of the words that I thought about a lot in this translation was 'khwab' for which I substituted 'dream' in English. I wanted to bring across the repetitive use of the noun from the Urdu original and reconstruct the open-ended possibilities of the dream sequence without trying to interpret the poem for the reader. 'Censorship' appealed for various reasons – the nostalgic quality which comes across in the latter half of the poem is characteristic of the migrant Urdu writer/poet; the incongruous juxtaposition of the mechanical functioning of the camera against the sublime depiction of nature; and the extinction of thought in an authoritarian climate. The most time-consuming and challenging part of the translation came in the last four lines of the poem where I found myself struggling with compound postpositions and a postpositional sequence. The Urdu postpositions work similarly to English prepositions.

The other four poems were part of later translations. 'Kare kos' established a link with a well known poem 'Bol' ('Speak') by Faiz Ahmed Faiz, which seeks to rouse the masses to claim their right of speech.[14] Naheed's poem is more personal, exploring the monological constructions of speech and comparing them with the ambiguities of the unsaid. For the very first line of the poem I chose a fairly wordy translation over Naheed's concise rendition. This was because of the interchangeability between word, letter, grammatical particle in the Urdu usage of 'harf'. I felt that translating 'harf' as 'a letter of the alphabet' rather than 'the word' was a better option as it allowed for a freer translation of the rest of the poem. I also wondered how best to translate the last three lines which included a couple of possessive adjectives, an oblique pronoun, and a postposition. I wanted to get the placement of the pronoun in just the right place without losing the rhythm of the original.

I was drawn to 'Apahaj ma mitti ki goldan jublee' and 'Apni jaisi aurat vazir-e azam se muqalima' during the fiftieth anniversary celebrations of Pakistani and Indian independence. The first had all the trappings of a big national poem and the traditional persona of the Progressive national poet arguing for social justice. I found this an easier poem to translate because of the use of direct speech at the beginning. In contrast to the crippled mother earth of 'Apahaj ma', 'Apni jaisi aurat' is in the voice of the female caretaker of the garden who uses her body as a marker of national oppression against women. There were a few idiomatic expressions that I had to think through in my translation, such as the line 'samp sampole ban bethi' which I have put across as 'Sticking like a snake to its newborn'. I found this a richer poem to translate in contrast to 'Apahaj ma' because the persona of the poet was less obtrusive. I did find that with the longer length of both these poems it was slightly easier to find my rhythm in the translation than in the shorter poems.

The last poem included here, 'Taliban se qibla ru guftagu', was a slightly more complex text to translate than the preceding two because of its word order, and the subtler nuances of a suggestive rather than prescriptive approach. One of the interesting variations in the original was the fluctuation between the third person pronoun 'ye' and 'vo'. Naheed uses 'vo' to refer to the distant Taliban and 'ye' for the closer community of girls. I kept that difference in my translation by using 'they' for the Taliban and 'these' for the girls. In the original she refers to the girls as both 'bachion' and 'larkian' which is difficult to reproduce as a single word in English so I used 'little girls' for the former and just 'girls' for the latter. Her use of 'bachion' is quite evocative because, although gendered as feminine, it conveys the asexual noun for girls in cultural usage as distinct from the pubescent associations of 'larki'.

As well as reconstructing some of the specificities involved in the translation process above, I have some reflective comments to make on my work as a translator. I have come to appreciate the knowledge that translation is not an isolated course of writing. Throughout I have had valuable and constructive advice from Urdu speakers, bilingual speakers, and English speakers, all of whom have generously given me their time by reading or listening to my translations and making insightful suggestions. Kishwar Naheed herself has been readily available for discussion with regards to the translations for which I am very grateful. I have found it difficult at times to stay faithful to my initial translations for various reasons, for example, sometimes I've missed the idiom, at other times I've strayed into interpretation, or just used the wrong word. For me, translation is a creative and collaborative process which allows me to work in the company of two immensely rich and varied languages with distinctive cultural formations.

NOTES

1. Kishwar Naheed, ed., *Women: Myth and Realities* (Lahore: Sang-e meel, 1993). There are some useful introductory collections available of Kishwar Naheed's poetry in English translation. The most recent is by Asif Furrukhi, ed., *The Distance of a Shout: Kishwar Naheed* (Karachi: Oxford University Press, 2001). Besides writing an insightful short introduction to this volume, Furrukhi has represented a wide selection of translators of Kishwar Naheed's poetry, such as Rukhsana Ahmad, Baidar Bakht, and Anisur Rahman. Literary criticism of Naheed's work has mostly been in Urdu and an important publication in this field is Asghar Nadeem Sayyid and Afzal Ahmad, eds, *Nae zamane ki birahan* (Lahore: Sang-e meel, 1990).
2. Kishwar Naheed, *Buri aurat ki katha* (*The narrative of a wretched woman*) (Lahore: Sang-e meel, 1993).
3. Kishwar Naheed, personal communication, 19 November 1996.
4. Naheed, *Buri aurat*, p. 23.
5. Naheed, personal communication, 19 November 1996.
6. Naheed, personal communication, 19 April 2000.
7. Kishwar Naheed, *Benam masafat* (*Anonymous journey*) (Lahore: Sang-e meel, 1991).
8. Kishwar Naheed, *Siyah hashiye men gulabi rang* (*Pink hue in a black margin*) (Lahore: Sang-e meel, 1986).
9. Kishwar Naheed, *Khiyali shakhs se muqabala* (*Contending with an imaginary person*) (Lahore: Sang-e meel, 1986), reprinted 1992.
10. Kishwar Naheed, *Main pehle janam men rat thi* (*I was night in my first incarnation*) (Lahore: Sang-e meel, 1998).
11. An earlier version of this translation appears in Asif Furrukhi, ed., *The Distance of a Shout: Kishwar Naheed*, p. 8.
12. An earlier version of this translation appears in *The SOAS Literary Review*, http://www.soas.ac.uk/soaslit/home.html. (01/11/99)
13. Amina Yaqin, 'The Intertextuality of Women in Urdu Literature: A Study of Fahmida Riaz and Kishwar Naheed' (unpublished doctoral thesis, University of London, School of Oriental and African Studies, 2001).
14. See Faiz Ahmed Faiz, 'Bol' ('Speak'), from *Naqsh-e faryadi* (*Remonstrance*), trans. Victor G Kiernan, *Poems by Faiz* (Lahore: Vanguard Books, 1971), pp. 86–9.

E. O. Hoppé Photographs the Recognized Face of Rabindranath Tagore

MICK GIDLEY

Emil Otto Hoppé (1878-1972) is now almost forgotten but, during the second two decades of the twentieth century, he was one of the most famous photographers in the world. He was born in Munich, moved to Britain in 1900, and became a professional, specializing first in portraiture, in 1907. By 1913 he was able to take over the prestigious Kensington house formerly owned by the Victorian painter Sir John Everett Millais. He used it as his studio for making his increasingly fashionable portraits of a galaxy of public figures, as a kind of salon, and as a gallery for a variety of small exhibitions, often credited to his pseudonym Dorien Leigh. F.T. Marinetti, the Italian Futurist, performed there, and *Joyzelle*, a short play by the Belgian Nobel laureate Maurice Maeterlinck, received its first English-language production there. Hoppé was so successful that in 1919, and annually for a time thereafter, he was able to operate a second portrait studio for several months of each year in New York City, and in 1927 he opened another studio in Berlin. And, all the while, from 1913, when he published his portfolio of *Studies from the Russian Ballet*, he worked on a series of illustrated books and portfolios, sometimes alone, sometimes in collaboration with others, as in the collections on modern writers compiled by Arthur St John Adcock, *Gods of Modern Grub Street* (1923) and *The Glory that was Grub Street* (1928). The summit of Hoppé's reputation as a portrait maker was probably reached in 1922, when he mounted a huge exhibition of his work at the Goupil Gallery, Regent Street, with a catalogue introduced by John Galsworthy, then at the height of *his* fame as the author of *The Forsyte Saga*.[1]

In the determination of meaning in photographic portraits, the role of the individual photographer is, without question, important. This is partly a matter of the artist's technique and aesthetic, as Hoppé himself acknowledged in 1923 when, in an essay comparing portraiture in painting and photography, he showed how the photographer must 'choose between the emphasising of lines and masses'; and it is partly, as

Hoppé also claimed, a more nebulous matter of deciding, in a moment, how to 'express' the 'impression' made upon the photographer by the sitter's qualities. Art historian Richard Brilliant, in his probing book *Portraiture*, allocates *the* most crucial role to the maker, privileging the maker's 'intentionality', not as a final cause of meaning but as the very occasion for any subsequent viewing and understanding.[2] But the photographic maker, while thus pivotal, is certainly not the only important determinant. Another, of course, is the wish and will of the sitter or subject. And when the subject is a well-known figure, a third determinant, as I will now try to show, is that obvious but puzzling entity 'the public'.

In speaking of his 1911 likeness of Henry James, Hoppé, with good evidence, said that, like the portraits he had made of Rudyard Kipling, Hilaire Belloc and Thomas Hardy, it had 'gained the distinction of becoming a kind of "recognised face" of the master'. The particular idea of recognition here is important. For a portrait to become the 'recognised face' it must command public acquiescence, even approval. Elsewhere Hoppé claimed that to be successful a portrait needed to uncover 'a personality that shall make *the spectator* feel the reality behind the portrait'. That is, in the case of – precisely – public figures, the generality of viewers are not passive. In the making and meaning of such images, the public is *constitutive*. This is partly a matter of circulation and exposure: in Belloc's case, by agreement between the writer and the photographer, Hoppé's portrait was the only one available for a time and, as such, it *had* to achieve recognition. But it was more often the case that a 'recognised face' would achieve large-scale circulation, its recognition factor encouraging distribution, its distribution in turn producing recognition. In the case of Kipling, for example, we know that Hoppé's likeness was so well recognized that its maker was able to turn it into a strong silhouette for one of *The Bookman*'s annual supplements: as a special feature of the 1913 Christmas edition, subscribers received a print of the silhouette ready for framing.[3]

In 1926, in *The Royal Magazine*, Hoppé published a choice set of his portraits, including George Bernard Shaw, Hardy, Galsworthy, and Benito Mussolini. Four of them depicted women: in haunting close-up, Lady Helen Lavery, the society beauty and wife of the painter Sir John Lavery; the Portuguese cellist Guilhermina Suggia, also the subject of one of Augustus John's most famous portraits; Ellen Terry, a major presence on the London stage for much of the seven decades preceding her death in 1928; and Gluck, the visionary artist and, later, designer.

The pictures were accompanied by 'As Others See Us', a brief article on portraiture by Hoppé; in this piece, as its title indicates, he was concerned to bring out not only what the photographic maker (as a potential 'other') could discern in and make of his subjects, but also what those 'Others' out there, the beholders, could 'see'. Thus viewers would recognize the 'sweetness' of Terry's personality, and that it was 'an emanation from all the parts she [had] played upon the stage of life, written in every gesture and line of her being', and they would, of course, see that Mussolini was 'an eager enthusiast, burning to impose his indomitable will upon the world'. Perhaps the constitutive role of viewers was most visible in the case of Gluck (who in 1895 had been born Hannah Gluckstein into the family that founded the Lyons catering empire and dynasty). Though Hoppé was personally well acquainted with Gluck, what he chose to stress in the commentary to her portrait in *The Royal Magazine* essay was, precisely, how *others* would see her: 'To look at the face of Gluck is to understand both her success as an artist and the fact that she dresses as a man. Originality, determination, strength of character and artistic insight are expressed in every line'.[4] The portrait, tellingly in profile, may indicate something of Gluck's own inner spirit – her 'determination' and so on – but it more forcefully calls for the public recognition and decoding of her demeanour and dress as lesbian.

In 1912, Rabindranath Tagore (1861-1941), already acknowledged in India as a major writer, mystic, and espouser of Indian self-governance through constitutional means, took a break from the management of his family estates and his school in Bengal to visit London. It was not his first visit: his father had sent him to England in 1878 to study law, an experience that had proved drab, unsuccessful, and unfulfilling, and in 1890 another, shorter visit was, at best, unremarkable. In 1912, however, partly through the famous good offices of the artist and educator William Rothenstein, the imperial capital became for Tagore a transformative site. He met a range of artists, intellectuals and political figures. With such helpful agents as W.B. Yeats and Ezra Pound, he gained an English-speaking readership for his translations of some of his poems that would very soon lead to the award of the Nobel Prize for literature. He delivered lectures, and – though he also encountered some racism – he was lionized, certainly more than was then the case at home. Max Beerbohm made him the subject of one of his celebrated caricatures: Tagore stands tall yet with an attitude of humility, his eyes closed in contemplation, and Rothenstein, in lotus-like position at the feet of the master, raises his hands in supplication; the caption says, 'Mr William Rothenstein warns Mr Tagore against being spoilt by occidental success'.[5]

Beerbohm obviously identified in Tagore a quality of ethereal innocence; but, if we read his caption fully, he also discerned a susceptibility to adulation – even a desire for it. It is clear that Tagore combined with his inner eye much visual awareness of the material, exterior world and its ways. 'This One in me knows the universe of the many,' he wrote. He frequently embellished the hand-written texts of his writings with expressive doodles and designs, turning them into truly illuminated manuscripts; he liked to sketch the world around him; and – though not until some years after 1912 – he also painted seriously, producing works in which, as in so many of his writings, the sights of the world are slightly abstracted and seem symbolically to intimate inner states. Yeats, in his 1913 Introduction to Tagore's *Gitanjali* (*Song Offerings*), felt that the Indian culture he encountered in *Gitanjali* shared with Nietzsche a belief in the causal relationship between the interior and the external; he wrote: 'we must not believe in the moral or intellectual beauty which does not impress itself upon physical things'. In later life, perhaps in 1934, Tagore used a crayon deliberately to play with, and even to deface, some photographs of himself, as if the 'One' in him was uncertain or even unhappy about his image; whether in 1912 he himself saw in his physical countenance an impression of his own contemplative inner 'beauty' we cannot know.[6]

But his biographers record many instances in which his physical appearance – his *looks*, not just his presence, so to speak – had a powerful effect on those he met. Leonard Elmhirst, whose work with Tagore in rural regeneration at Sriniketan inspired him to co-found Dartington, Devon, as a school with associated industries, admired Tagore's 'magnificent physique'. Poet Robert Bridges, himself regarded as a handsome man, said that 'when [Tagore] came into the room he made us all look almost mean'. Frances Cornford, Darwin's granddaughter, wrote from Cambridge to Rothenstein: 'I must … tell you… what a wonderful thing it has been to see Tagore … He *is* like a saint, and the beauty and dignity of his whole being is wonderful to remember'. Some commentators have noted, understandably, that this kind of near stereotyping of Tagore as the sage of the East was – or became – irksome to him. But in 1912, when Cornford met him, Tagore certainly realized the visual appeal of his striking features and got himself frequently photographed. Given his towering height, flowing robes, and the glistening waves of his beard and long hair, there is no doubt that metropolitan but insular Londoners found him an exotic figure. The press, ostensibly referring to his verses, would speak of people falling 'under the spell of this Indian poet'. Tagore experienced a similar reception when he travelled on to the United States: Mary Lago, Tagore's most devoted Western scholar, has noted that the press there stressed his appearance as 'The poet who looked like a poet'.[7]

But Tagore was not simply the object of the camera's gaze, a famous personage chased down by newsmen and caught in the glare of flash – though, obviously, he did not entirely escape such treatment. Rather, until the mid-1920s he himself deliberately visited the studios of several significant photographic portrait-makers, whether in Calcutta, London or Los Angeles. The results show that Tagore actively contributed to the construction of his own image. Hoppé's studio, in 1912 at 59 Baker Street, was one of the premises he frequented. Hoppé – who was able regularly to place his portraits of authors in both literary outlets, such as *The Bookman* (which was edited by his collaborator Arthur St John Adcock), and general illustrated middlebrow journals, such as *The Graphic* – made several portraits of Tagore, probably during a single sitting. It has not proved possible to trace their complete circulation, but it is certain that they worked to augment the fame that Tagore's writing was rapidly acquiring in the world beyond India. (It was only the following year that Tagore became the first non-'white' and first non-Western author to be awarded the Nobel Prize.) In 1922, when Hoppé mounted his Goupil show, one of his portraits of Tagore [Plate 1] was prominently featured. It presents the poet full-faced, strong and intense yet exposed and ethereal. In 1945, when Hoppé published his autobiography, he also included another of his earlier portraits of Tagore, this time slightly confined within the close frame, an effect that emphasizes the impact of his presence [Plate 2].[8]

In 1921, very much acting as an author, Hoppé joined the newly established PEN (Poets, Playwrights, Essayists, Editors, and Novelists) Club. He also made an arrangement with PEN that when prominent writers came to London from abroad, they should be sent round to his studio – and copies of images thus made were to be displayed in the PEN committee rooms. But this was not the way Hoppé resumed his acquaintance with Tagore. Rather, in the later 1920s, he became increasingly committed to travel, to travel writing and to travel photography, so that in this phase of his career portraiture became more of a tributary to his nomadic assignments than a vocation in its own

Plate 1. (left) Rabindranath Tagore, c. 1920, by E. O. Hoppé (courtesy Curatorial Assistance, Pasadena, California)

Plate 2. Rabindranath Tagore, c. 1920 (or 1929), by E. O. Hoppé (courtesy Curatorial Assistance, Pasadena, California)

right. A kind of news photography became Hoppé's dominant mode, in that much of the travel income derived from payments for items he placed in the middlebrow illustrated press and from royalties from a series of travel books, most notably *Round the World with a Camera* (1934). It was in this more reportorial role that, late in 1929, he visited Tagore's India. Together with his son Frank, he toured the length and breadth of the subcontinent, taking pictures of palaces in Udaipur, pilgrims in Benares, and snake charmers everywhere. In the course of these peregrinations, Hoppé journeyed to Santiniketan ('Abode of Peace') to experience at first hand the ashram, the educational community, and the Sriniketan agricultural regeneration projects initiated by 'The Poet'. Hoppé asserted in his autobiography that he had 'received an invitation to spend one week at the home of the poet'. Treating the visit in his usual way, he then annotated his photographs and wrote up his experience. At the same time, Hoppé seems to have taken his membership of PEN seriously, and suggested in correspondence with its secretary that a branch of the international organization should be started in India, especially for 'native writers', and claimed that, due to his own missionary work, Tagore had agreed to join.[9]

The interest of Hoppé's account in *Round the World with a Camera* of his visit to Tagore and the renowned community he led at Santiniketan is, really, that it is so consensual, even undistinguished. It is typical travel writing of the time. The three pages of the book devoted to Santiniketan concentrate on the Visva-Bharati, the 'All-India World University' that Tagore had founded, briefly delineating the fundamental principles at work in this overtly internationalist enterprise devoted both to melding the beliefs of East and West and to encouraging a deeper appreciation of the humble folkways of India itself. It also evokes the atmosphere – the natural colours and aromas – of this 'University of the wilds' and introduces a gallery of its characters, whether Indian students and administrators or imported European and American devotees and professors. But, of Tagore himself, we get only a quotation that could have been taken from a prospectus for the community ('The spirit of sacrifice and comradeship … the disinterested desire to help others, which the boys here have developed, are rare traits even in children who have had better opportunities') – in fact, it was taken from such a prospectus. And even of author and photographer Hoppé himself at Santiniketan, or in India generally, we learn little of substance. What we do learn fits all too well the contours of the typical metropolitan citizen of the Empire at that time in the early 1930s. For example, the text completely ignores Tagore's belief in self-determination for India, despite his distrust in political nationalism, and his high regard – if only intermittent support – for Gandhi in his leadership of the struggle for independence.[10]

The following is typical of the considered views presented in *Round the World with a Camera*:

> In common with many other travellers who have spent much time in India, I am convinced that any system of Home Rule will never succeed, religions and interests are far too diversified and, even though in Calcutta I was present at a dinner at which the guests included two Hindus, a Mohammedan, a Parsee and two Christians and quite amicably we discussed religion, I found everywhere, from the Royal Palaces and Princes downwards, that the intelligent Indians do not want the influence of the British Raj to be withdrawn; they appreciate our genius for government, and although there may be domestic anomalies – such, for instance, as the fact that an Indian may not be a member of the Stock Exchange in Calcutta, having to sit outside upon the steps, while an Armenian jew [sic] is accepted – they realise that our directing hand is genuinely for their good and that we do not interfere with their age-old customs.

This passage does *not*, after all, constitute much of a revelation: in its totality – that is, including its troubling overt and almost casual anti-Armenianism and anti-Semitism – it represents, as Hoppé himself seemed to acknowledge ('in common with many other travellers'), an assumed *consensual* viewpoint. The writer and the writing simply take for granted that readers will share such opinions, opinions that were, indeed, all too common in 1930s Britain. It is as if the passage merely transmits the prevalent ideology. This is made even more obvious in the next paragraph, where Hoppé immediately contradicts himself by saying that when the Raj *did* interfere with 'age-old' customs, as in the passage of the Child Marriage Restraint Bill of 1929, this, too, was really for the benefit of Indians themselves. In *Mother India* (1927), to which Hoppé refers, the American journalist Katherine Mayo had excoriated child marriage – mainly because of what she saw as its consequent sexual abuse – and her highly contentious yet influential book had resulted in the Child Marriage Restraint Bill. In conventionally colonialist fashion, Hoppé asserts that he himself knew of girls aged only nine being forced into consummation of marriage and, entirely ignoring Tagore's own deep hostility to Mayo – Tagore believed she had knowingly traduced his views on Indian marital customs – he looks to Tagore, as a source of 'enlightenment', to lead India away from such practices in slow, serene steps, and to advance the nation towards what 'our' (presumably British) genius for government can approve. Moreover, in this polemical discussion, perhaps to reinforce Tagore's status as a force for approved enlightenment, Hoppé reassigned to the poet the knighthood he had renounced in 1919 as a protest against the then recent British massacre at Amritsar.[11]

The passage of *Round the World with a Camera* just quoted, as well as ignoring certain of Tagore's views, also concealed something about Hoppé: he had an undisclosed personal investment both in the Raj generally and, if in some tension with prevailing imperialist attitudes, in the successful circulation of Katherine Mayo's views of Indian society, including its marriage patterns. At the very period in which he was writing *Round the World* he was also profitably engaged in providing a considerable number of images for Mayo's 1935 book, *The Face of Mother India*, a pictorial popularization of the earlier *Mother India*.[12] It has not been possible to discover for certain Tagore's response to *The Face of Mother India*, in particular to the quarter of its images specifically attributable to Hoppé, but it is likely that it followed the pattern of his irritation with Mayo's earlier book, which he saw as the product of a prejudiced Western traveller's fleeting engagement with a profound and ancient civilization, itself divided and doubtful as to what of its varied culture to conserve from the past into the future.

All told, Hoppé's images and words grant no unique or new revelations into the many sides of Tagore – or, indeed, into the complexities of Indian civilization. Rather, what we can take from these representations, whether offered in photographs or words, is Tagore's 'recognised' face. Thus, nearly twenty pages after his description of Santiniketan, Hoppé could write in the closing section of the Indian chapter of *Round the World with a Camera*: 'I came away [from India] with a memory of one of the world's greatest dreamers, with his long flowing beard, surrounded by his young disciples, whose message might mean resurrection for the million denizens of this human jungle, which is India' – and could do so without any need to re-use the poet's name. Moreover, during the Santiniketan visit in 1929 Hoppé had made precisely *that* image of the poet, complete – as the framing and positioning tell us – with a 'disciple' beside him as scribe [Plate 3]. Here, as elsewhere in Hoppé's prodigious output, what is important about his work is that it grants some purchase on – in that the photographs enable us, literally, to see – the *typical* assumptions of the (then) dominant culture. The 'recognised face' has become, in effect, a mask hiding the inner 'One'. We know from the biographies devoted to him that Tagore

*Plate 3. Rabindranath Tagore, with student or colleague, 1929, by E.O. Hoppé
(courtesy Curatorial Assistance, Pasadena, California)*

was a 'myriad-minded man', as Krishna Dutta and Andrew Robinson claim, but Hoppé – whether in 1912, 1929 or 1934 (the dating is ultimately unimportant) – always went for the same, if ageing, recognized face.[13] Though Tagore certainly helped to determine this face and registered his powerful presence, the results were not 'impressions' of the inner man – or, even, exterior views based on intimacy – but the received vision of the time, as seen through Western eyes.

NOTES

The author is grateful for financial support from the AHRB, The Leverhulme Trust, and The British Academy.

1. Biographical information on Hoppé is based on his own writings, including his autobiography, *Hundred Thousand Exposures* (London and New York: Focal Press, 1945), corrected and augmented by primary research, especially in the archives held by the E.O. Hoppé Trust, Curatorial Assistance, Pasadena, California (hereafter CA). The catalogue of his major show is *New Camera Work by E.O. Hoppé* (London: William Marchant & Co., The Goupil Gallery, 1922).

2. Hoppé, 'The Portrait in Painting and Photography', *Drawing and Design* NS 3 (August 1923), 570-573 (p. 572) and Hoppé, 'Maurice Maeterlinck: An Impressionistic Photograph', *The Bookman*, 46 (May 1914), 85-86 (p. 86). Richard Brilliant, *Portraiture* (London: Reaktion, 1991), especially the introduction.

3. For Hoppé on James, see *Hundred Thousand Exposures*, p. 48, where he misdates the portrait to 1915 (James himself inscribed the verso of a print of this portrait, now in the Houghton Library at Harvard, with the date January 1, 1912; Houghton 2001-624F). Hoppé, 'The Psychology of the Camera Portrait', *Colour*, 1 (August 1914), 40. For Kipling silhouette, see *The Bookman*, Special Supplement, Christmas 1913.

4. Hoppé, 'As Others See Us', *The Royal Magazine*, 57 (December 1926), 107-114; quotation about Gluck, p. 110.

5. Biographical information on Tagore in this article is taken from various sources, most significantly Krishna Dutta and Andrew Robinson, *Rabindranath Tagore: The Myriad-Minded Man* (London: Bloomsbury, 1995). The 1912 visit is well conveyed through primary documents in *Imperfect Encounter: Letters of William Rothenstein and Rabindranath Tagore 1911-1941*, ed. Mary M. Lago (Cambridge, MA: Harvard University Press, 1972), pp. 37-131. Beerbohm's caricature is reproduced in both Dutta and Robinson, after p. 304, and *Imperfect Encounter*, p. 205.

6. The Tagore quotation is from his book of essays *Creative Unity* (London: Macmillan, 1926), p. v. For Tagore's visual art, see *Rabindranath Tagore: A Celebration of His Life and Work* (London: Rabindranath Tagore Festival, 1986), a collection of essays and illustrations to accompany a travelling exhibition of his paintings. Yeats, 'Introduction', *Gitanjali* (London: Macmillan, 1913), p. ix. The photographic portraits that Tagore doodled with (c.1934) are reproduced in Dutta and Robinson, after p. 368. Tagore himself often wrote about the correspondence – or lack of such – between the 'outward life and the inner', for example, in *My Reminiscences* (London: Macmillan, 1917), p. 212 and *passim*.

7. Elmhirst, 'Preface', in *Rabindranath Tagore, Pioneer in Education: Essays and Exchanges*

between Rabindranath Tagore and L.K. Elmhirst (London: John Murray for Visva-Bharati, 1961), p. 9. Bridges is quoted in Edward Thompson, *Rabindranath Tagore: Poet and Dramatist* (Oxford: Oxford University Press, 2nd rev. ed., 1948), p. 286. Lago quotes Cornford in the course of a brief discussion of the stereotyping of Tagore *as the Orient* (*Imperfect Encounter*, p. 19, my emphasis). The press quotation is from Krishna Kripalani, *Rabindranath Tagore: A Biography* (London: Oxford University Press, 1962), p. 223; many more such remarks could be cited. Mary Lago, 'Restoring Rabindranath Tagore', in *Rabindranath Tagore: Perspectives in Time*, eds. Lago and Ronald Warwick (London: Macmillan, 1989), pp. 4-25 (p. 16).

8. The Tagore archives at Santiniketan contain numerous portraits of the poet and very many of these have been reproduced in the voluminous literature devoted to him; the stamps and studio insignia of their makers (such as 'Bourne & Shepherd, Calcutta' or 'Edward S. Curtis, Los Angeles') are often visible. Hoppé's numbering and dating of his negatives, though well preserved by CA, is not always easy to follow, and it may be that the Tagore portrait in the Goupil show (listed as No. 42 in *New Camera Work by E. O. Hoppé*) was made during a Tagore visit later than 1912 (a copy print in the collections of the National Portrait Gallery, London, is dated 1920). Hoppé claimed that the portrait of Tagore that he reproduced in *Hundred Thousand Exposures*, p. 58, was made in 1929, but he was often forgetful about dates and this dating is uncertain.

9. Information on Hoppé's relationship with PEN is taken from Hoppé's correspondence with figures at PEN, in particular a letter to Herman Ould, January 12, 1930, PEN Recip, Harry Ransom Humanities Research Center, University of Texas, Austin. For Tagore's invitation, see *Hundred Thousand Exposures*, p. 48. Typical of the illustrated articles Hoppé produced in India is 'A Maharana Gives a Studio Sitting', *The Graphic*, 19 April 1930, p. 123. One of his articles on Santiniketan is 'Practical Idealists: The Tagore Family', *The Bookman*, 79 (November 1930), 112-113; the archive at CA contains similar typescripts of others.

10. *Round the World with a Camera* (London: Hutchinson, 1934), pp. 116-120. The quotation from Tagore (p. 118) seems to follow verbatim a publicity brochure published by the university, *Visva-Bharati: My School* (n.d.), found in the Hoppé archives at CA. A succinct account of Tagore's views on the politics of nationalism is Ray Monk, 'Tagore on Nationalism' in *Rabindranath Tagore: A Celebration*, pp. 26-29.

11. The quotation is from *Round the World with a Camera*, pp. 116-117. Mayo, *Mother India* (New York and London: Harpers, 1927). Dutta and Robinson offer an interesting discussion of Tagore's reactions to Mayo, pp. 279-284.

12. Mayo, *The Face of Mother India* (New York and London: Harper and Brothers, 1935); Hoppé was the major photographic contributor to this book. The Katherine Mayo Collection, Manuscripts and Archives, Yale University Library, New Haven, CT, contains much routine picture acquisition correspondence between Mayo and Hoppé and Dorien Leigh Ltd, notably M.E. Chickall of Dorien Leigh to Mayo, 23 March 1935 and Mayo to 'Miss Leigh', 16 April 1935.

13. *Round the World with a Camera*, p. 134. Dutta and Robinson, *Rabindranath Tagore* (1995).

A Cat in the Agraharam
(AGRAHARATHIL POONAI)

DILIP KUMAR
TRANSLATED FROM TAMIL BY SUBASHREE KRISHNASWAMY

'Can't this wretched old creature die? This is the seventh time,' cursed Babli Paati in Gujarati through clenched teeth.

Madhuri, who came out of the kitchen, understood immediately, 'Has it drunk it all up and slipped away, again?'

The old lady screamed, 'Evil creature, can't move this side–that side for even a minute in this house ...' Suddenly and very skilfully she changed tack and addressed her daughter-in-law in chaste, grammatically perfect language, 'That's all very well, but what may I ask was Your Highness doing that you didn't even notice a cat come in?'

Madhuri knew that the old lady's question warranted no answer. She was the one who had ordered a while ago, 'While I finish the puja, mix the gram flour and make the drumstick curry.' Surely the old lady would have sniffed the heavenly aroma of roasted gram flour. Holding her veil in place between two fingers, Madhuri stood by the door of the kitchen as was her wont, and in accustomed silence.

'What are you staring at?' said Babli Paati. 'Go bring me another cup of milk. We have to do something about this wretched cat as soon as Nattu comes home.'

As soon as they heard the hoo-ha in Babli Paati's house, Gopal Bhai who was rinsing his underwear and Sharada Behn who was washing vessels in the open verandah on the first floor peeped out. 'Cunning cat, just disappeared in a second,' commiserated Sharada Behn, clapping her hand on her chin. Babli Paati turned towards the puja shelf without uttering a word.

The Ekambareswarar agraharam edged the temple tank on three sides, like the Tamil letter 'pa', behind the Ekambareswarar temple on Mint Street. Cats generally never entered the agraharam. In fact, you could say that no member of the feline species had entered the precincts in the last fifty or sixty years. The residents had run across the creatures now and then only on Mint Street, Govindappa Naicken Street, or at

Kondithoppu. It was for philosophical rather than environmental reasons that they never entered the agraharam – the majority of the residents were Pushti Margi Vaishnavaites! After all, there was no guarantee that the esteem in which the Tenkalai Vaishnavaites held a cat would be shared by the Pushti Margis. Yes, it was true that the Pushti Margis whose main deity was Balakrishna – Baby Krishna – loved all creatures, great and small. But it was the cow, which munched on polythene bags and cinema posters and dropped dung tastelessly all over the place, that they cherished above all other things. After all, Krishna Paramatma himself was a cowherd, wasn't he? Somehow cats too intuitively comprehended this great truth – that is, till the month of April.

It was in the month of May that the above-mentioned old cat casually strolled into the agraharam and, funnily enough, nobody even stumbled across it. The cat was first spotted in the front room of No. 9 on the first floor of building No. 25 where twenty-four Gujarati families lived. When Babli Paati who had kept ready the cup of milk for the puja nipped in for a minute to wash the betel leaves to make beeda for 'Balakrishna', it gracefully strolled in, fearlessly slurped up the entire cup of milk, and nonchalantly walked away as if nothing had happened.

Babli Paati was in a quake. She could only blather loudly in Gujarati, 'Arré ... arré ... biladi ... Madhu, biladi ... Madhu, biladi ...' On hearing her shriek, the creature turned calmly, stood still for a couple of minutes in the middle of the hall, outstaring Paati, eye for eye, and then sauntered away. Paati grabbed the madi pole, specially kept against the door to pull down ritually pure clothes from the washing line, and flung it in the cat's direction, but it vanished nimbly.

At first, Madhuri, who came running in with wet hands, could only smile looking at her mother-in-law's disturbed countenance. But she didn't dare laugh. Paati, clearly overwrought, stood still, pursing her lips. 'Never mind, Ba, forget it, it's only a dumb creature,' comforted Madhuri.

'Chee, shut up, you barren donkey,' spat out the old lady. Madhuri felt belittled.

Babli Paati was blessed with an excellent constitution. A small grey bun, a long beaky nose, slim egg-shaped glasses, tulasi beads round her neck. Her skin, with its rosy tinge, shone like a ripe fruit.

She would get up at the crack of dawn – at four in the morning, bathe, don a white saree, and go to the Haveli five buildings away – with a bare forehead, mind you – and come back only at ten. She would then start her puja routine for the family gods. First, she would settle herself down in front of the glass-panelled teak almirah, inside which idols dressed in silk and gold nestled against tiny mattresses. Following a strict order, she would carefully take the idols out, one by one, remove their clothes and bathe them. Then, wiping them dry with a velvet cloth, she would reach for the biscuit tin filled to the brim with fresh clothes and dress them up painstakingly. The chief idol, Balakrishna, sported a thumb-sized silk zari cap as well. Only after dotting the gods with kumkumam would she place them back on the mattresses. Then, on a wooden plank in front of the almirah, a big thali would be placed, tiny cups containing all kinds of food arranged in a perfect circle. One small cup was specially meant for mini beedas. She would then perform the arati, ring the bell, sing a bhajan to the tune of Jai Jagdish Haré, and close the almirah behind her. Only then would she consider taking even a sip of cold water.

Babli Paati was well known in the agraharam. On spiritual matters she was an authority and, especially on Pushti Margi rites, there was none to dispute her scholarship. She was well informed on all ceremonial and remedial rules — what fast to be observed for a particular problem, what good fortune followed which puja, what was to be done on navaratri, or for a death anniversary, marriage, bangle-ceremony, bridal-play or any other occasion. She could recite the Bhagavatam back to front. Even the subtlest of metaphysical details didn't escape her, she could argue convincingly. (A few weeks ago a girl researching on Pushti Marg came all the way from Baroda and had her doubts cleared up.) Brahmin priests officiating the functions she attended were known to cringe in her presence.

Even though Babli Paati was much admired and feted, her daughter-in-law Madhuri stubbornly refused to acknowledge her greatness. As far as she was concerned the old lady was a wily one. Her feelings notwithstanding, she was unhappy that her mother-in-law's puja continued to be defiled. This was what happened the last six times — she would take the wick, mix the dhal rice, cut the fruit, disappear inside for a minute to fetch the matchbox, and, in the blink of an eye, as if preordained, the clever cat would finish the job and be gone.

That evening, as soon as Babli Paati's son Nattu (alias Natwarlal) returned from office, she started complaining about the cat. 'Nattu, I don't know what you will do or how you will do it, but somehow get rid of that wretched old thing.'

Nattu had the looks of a well-built policeman but he was a simpleton.

He was scared to even raise his voice. He maintained the 'no. 2' accounts for a Marwadi merchant in Chembudas Street. His official 'no.1' salary amounted to a thousand rupees, but he was given another thousand on the side from the 'no. 2' account. Idle chitchat, gossip, beedi-cigarette, cinema-drama, he had none of these vices. He kept to himself, did his job and nothing more. He would come back from the office, change his clothes, leave for the Haveli, and return only at eight. On Saturdays, at about ten in the night, he would attend bhajan sessions. On Gujarati New Year's day Madhuri would be taken to the cinema or the beach.

'What are you saying, Ba? It's a sin to kill a cat,' he said, in a horrified voice.

'Ada, saltless fellow, am I asking you to kill the cat! Just chase it away somewhere. As if I don't know it's a sin to kill a cat. He's trying to teach me ...'

'How can I chase it away? In order to chase it, I must first spot it, no? It's all because of your carelessness. Placing the cup of milk in the middle of the floor well before it is time, and announcing to the world at large that you're going to do puja, and then ending up shouting hai, hai!'

'That's enough. Don't be too smart. I suppose I must learn from you how to do a puja.'

'Ok, ok, leave it. I'll tell Suri. He's the right one for such a job.'

'Have you misplaced your brain? That evil fellow Suri of all people! That barbaric good-for-nothing might really finish off the cat. Be careful.'

'You don't worry about that. I'll see to everything,' said Nattu firmly.

Suri was Babli Paati's younger brother Ranjit Singh's eldest son Surendran. A useless unemployed layabout. A happy-go-lucky fellow who joyfully roamed the streets, a gaggle of friends trailing behind him, always brightly dressed, his jaws forever masticating Calcutta paan. He could swear with amazing facility in both Gujarati and Tamil. There were two things he hated: the rich and God. But he was bound by love. A well-meaning ruffian, he took it upon himself to dispense justice in the agraharam. It was his firm belief in the axiom 'caste second to justice' that made him fling the cycle of an elderly Gujarati gentleman, who picked a quarrel with a young flower-seller, into the moss and sludge-ridden temple tank.

Madhuri, who was making the dough for the chapati in the kitchen, heard the mother and son. She thought of the white cat – it looked pathetic, ready to die, with its droopy face, peeled skin, patchy hair and all. Whenever it stared intently, she almost expected it to speak. When

Babli Paati wasn't around, it would appear by the front door with a plaintive meow, its jaws wide open. Madhuri never failed to give it milk. In a way, there wasn't much difference between herself and the cat, she mused. Like the creature, she too lived a very furtive life. Did it have any kittens? In its youth it would certainly have had a litter or two. Or was it also barren? The small triumphs in its miserable little life could be compared to hers. A cup of milk for the cat amounted to a saree for herself, or perhaps an evening by the beach, or a Hindi film. Like the cat, she too would one day turn old and decrepit. Like the cat, she too would be all alone in this world. After all, old age did not afford any opportunity for love. Was it available in such plenty anyhow that it could be showered so easily? If so, in whose heart could it be found? Babli Paati's? Her husband Nattu's? Where was it hidden, this absurdity called love? In the cat's dull yellow eyes?

She banged the dough angrily against the plate.

To Nattu, the cat affair didn't appear important. He forgot about it immediately. Only when he caught sight of Suri on his way back from the Haveli did it come to mind. 'You've told me, no, Nattu Bhai, you can assume that the job is done,' said Suri enthusiastically in Gujarati. 'Just say the word and I will pack it off, not only from the agraharam but to America itself.'

Nattu was perturbed, 'No, no, don't do all that. Just see that it doesn't appear near No. 25. That's enough.'

'Done, Nattu Bhai, done,' said Suri firmly in English.

The next day Paati's son-in-law Hansraj landed from Kochi on account of work. He was like that – always appearing out of the blue, without a word. Babli Paati thought very highly of her son-in-law. The only thing she didn't like in him was his habit of taking snuff. He was only thirty-eight, but he looked like a sadhu in pants, with his Bhagavatar hairstyle, luxuriant beard, moustache and all. It was said he turned like that only after his marriage.

Babli Paati's daughter Nimmu had been an ordinary enough young girl but, suddenly, after marriage, she started to bloat. At first, everyone thought it was a sign of a happy marriage but, when she ballooned bizarrely, they knew something was wrong. Over and above his inherited wealth, Hansraj earned a handsome income and spent money on his wife like water. But to no avail. Unbelievably fat by the time she turned thirty, she required two-and-a-quarter metres just for a blouse! There wasn't place for anyone else if she got into an auto. Merely taking ten steps made her pant and gasp for breath. At home she went about her work either sitting or crawling. Hansraj redesigned the entire kitchen to suit her needs.

Nimmu wasn't one to worry unduly about her obesity. With a ready smile she lavished affection on whoever came her way. Even people who had known her for only ten minutes became extremely attached to her. She graciously tended to guests, crawling in and out of the kitchen like a small child. Doctors warned that she had, at the most, only ten more years to live. She often joked loudly, 'When I die, I will need sixteen people to carry me.' To Hansraj, Nimmu was everything, his whole life.

The cat didn't come anywhere near Babli Paati's house the week Hansraj stayed with them. In fact, in the excitement of ministering to her son-in-law, Paati forgot about the animal.

When Hansraj was starting for home, she packed a big tin full of Nimmu's favourite snacks. 'See if you can bring Nimmu for Diwali this year?' she said.

'You are aware of her condition. If she is to come, I have to bring her in a van. Why don't you come instead to Kochi for a week? It will be a change for you.'

'What change? Will it happen if you say so? If I go away, who will look after the house? She's hardly competent. Even Governor Patwari can take some time off, I can't.'

Noticing Nattu by the door, Paati said, 'Ok, you have to go. Nattu has brought an auto.' She came up to the door to see Hansraj off, thought of her daughter, and swallowed her tears. 'I'll take leave, sister,' said Hansraj to Madhuri.

Ten days passed. All of a sudden, on a Sunday, Suri appeared at No. 25 with the cat. As soon as he reached the door, young and old crowded around him. The cat lay nestled against his chest like a baby, tucked firmly under his left hand.

Unable to believe her eyes, Paati said, 'What a devious creature. The thieving wretch is fawning all over you.'

'That's Suri, for sure. In the last ten days it has consumed five litres of milk and eight double omelettes. Is it easy to cast a spell on a cat? I just thought I'd show it to you before I take it away. Tell me, Foi Ba, where shall I leave it – Tiruvattiyur or Tiruvanmyur?'

The more Suri stroked the cat with his right hand the more it wriggled coyly like a shy bride. Babli Paati, having gazed intently at the cat, announced with an air of sudden decision, 'Dei, Suri, don't run away. I'll be back in a minute.' She went in to search for the snuffbox that her son-in-law had left behind.

She returned quickly to the door, signalled covertly for Suri to come closer, and in a low voice urged him to bring the cat near her. Clutching on to its stomach, Suri stretched the cat in front of her. Paati quickly brought her closed fist from her hip, in a trice opened her palm, and pressed the entire contents of the box on to the cat's nose.

In the next instant, as if struck by lightning, the cat jerked out of Suri's hand and lay supine on the ground, completely disoriented. Time and again it tried to get up, only to wobble around, crashing against the tap, the drain, and the bathroom door. The strange cry that emanated from it was harrowing. Buckling down on its feet, it turned its head this way and that, and sneezed pitifully.

Babli Paati dusted her hands. The remaining snuff blew in the wind, and everyone gathered there, including Suri, started to sneeze. A few bystanders, children and men who were standing a little further away, laughed uproariously at the sight of a cat sneezing and tottering. The cat somehow got on to the ledge of the first floor, scaled the wall, sneezed yet again and fell down with a thud. Then, picking itself up slowly, it left the building.

Heaping obscenities at the cackling bystanders, Suri ran after the cat.

Suddenly there was dead silence and the crowd dispersed. Paati who turned to go in found Madhuri standing still in the middle of the hall. She quickly lowered her head and went past her daughter-in-law.

That evening she had a guest. Babli Paati began: 'What Pushti Marg says ...'

Notes

Agraharam: the area leading off a temple, where Brahmins usually live.
Paati: grandmother, also used to address elderly women.
Biladi: cat.
Haveli: temple.
Foi Ba: aunt.

Electrification

TRANSLATED BY ROBERT CHANDLER

MIKHAIL MIKHAILOVICH ZOSHCHENKO

What, brothers, is today's most fashionable word?

Today's most fashionable word of all is, of course, electrification.

Lighting up Soviet Russia with light, without doubt, is a matter of massive importance. No one can argue with that. But it does, for the time being, have its downside. I'm not saying, comrades, that it costs too much. It costs money – that's all. No, I'm saying something different.

What I'm saying is this:

I was living, comrades, in a huge building. The whole of this building ran on paraffin. Some of us had lamps, some – cans of oil with a wick. The poorest had to make do with church candles. Life wasn't easy.

And then they start to install light.

First it's the house manager. Light's up his room – and that's that. A quiet fellow, doesn't let on what he's thinking. Though he wanders about a bit strangely and keeps absent-mindedly blowing his nose.

But he doesn't let on what he's thinking.

Then in comes my dear wife, Yelizaveta Ignatyevna Prokhorova. Says we should illuminate the apartment.

'Everyone,' she says, 'is installing light. The director himself has installed light,' she says.

So – of course – we do the same.

Light is installed, the apartment illuminated – heavens above! What foulness and filth!

Till then, you went to work in the morning, you came back in the evening, you drank down your tea and you went to bed. You never saw a thing with just paraffin. But now, with illumination – you see wallpaper flapping off the wall, and somebody's beaten-up slipper lying about on the floor. You see a bedbug trotting along, trying to get away from the light. An old rag here, a gob of spit there, a fag end, a flea frisking about...

Heavens above! It's enough to make you call the night watchman. Such a sight is sad to see.

In our room, for instance, we had a couch. I'd always thought it wasn't a bad couch – even quite a good couch! In the evenings I used to sit on it. But now with this electricity – heavens above! Some couch! Bits sticking up, bits hanging down, bits falling out. How can I sit on such a couch? My soul protests.

No, I think, I don't live in luxury. Everything's revolting to look at. And everything I do goes wrong.

Then I see dear Yelizaveta Ignatyevna. She looks sad. She's muttering away to herself, tidying things up in the kitchen.

'What,' I ask, 'are you so sad about, dear wife?'

She throws up her hands in despair.

'I had no idea, my dear man,' she says, 'what a shabby life I've been living.'

I look at our bits and pieces. Not so great, I think. Foulness and filth. Rags of one kind and rags of another kind. All flooded with light and staring you in the eye.

So I start to get a bit down in the mouth, you might say, when I come back home in the evenings.

I come in. I switch on the light. I briefly admire the lamp, then bury my nose in the pillow.

Then I think again. I get my pay. I buy whitewash, I mix it up – and I set to work. I tear off wallpaper, I stamp out bedbugs, I sweep away cobwebs. I sort out the couch, I paint, I adorn – my soul sings and rejoices.

I did well. But not that well. It was in vain, dear brothers, that I blew all that money. My wife cut the wires.

'Light,' she says, 'makes life seem horribly shabby. Why,' she says, 'shine light on our poverty? The bedbugs will die of laughter.'

I beg her. I argue arguments with her. No use.

'You can move,' she says, 'to another apartment. I don't want,' she says, 'to live with light. I've no money,' she says, 'to renovate and renew.'

But how could I move, comrades, after spending a fortune on whitewash? I gave in.

Light's all very well, brothers, but it's not easy to live with.

First published 1924

Simplicity of Souls
TRANSLATED BY ROBERT CHANDLER

MIKHAIL MIKHAILOVICH ZOSHCHENKO

Perhaps you remember when the Negroes visited. Last year. A black minstrel company.

Those Negroes were really extremely happy with our hospitality. Yes, they really praised our culture and all our undertakings in general.

The only thing they weren't happy about was how we move around on the streets.

'It's hard,' they kept saying, 'to get about. Everybody pushes and shoves and treads on your heels.'

Well, these Negroes, of course, have been spoiled by European civilization and they're well and truly, how can I put it, out of practice. Give them a couple of years here and they'll lose their rough edges and be treading on everyone's feet themselves. And that's a fact.

Still, we do tread on feet. There's no getting away from it. We have that failing.

But it only happens, I want to tell the Negroes, because of our simplicity of soul. There's no malice aforethought. You tread on a foot – and walk on. Simple as that.

The other day I myself trod on a citizen's foot. The citizen, you see, was walking down the street. A broad-shouldered, strong-looking lad.

He walks and walks. I walk behind him. And he walks in front. Just a step away.

And we're walking along, you know, very nicely. Correctly. Not treading on one another's feet. Not flinging our arms about. He walks. And I walk. We really aren't, you could say, bothering one another at all. We're in step. Our souls, in a word, in tune. Joy in our hearts.

And I think:

'The man's walking splendidly. Evenly. Not kicking about. Anyone else would be getting under your feet, but he strides calmly forward.'

And all of a sudden, I don't know why, I was gazing at some beggar. Or maybe cabdriver.

And, as I was gazing at this beggar, I trod with all my weight on the foot of my friend in front. On his heel. And just above.

I trod on his foot, I have to say, seriously. With all possible force.

And for a moment I even froze in fear.

I stopped.

I even – I was so startled – didn't say 'sorry'.

This dear man, I thought, will turn round and take a swing at me. He'll belt me one on the ear: 'Walk normally, mutton-head!'

I froze, I tell you, in fear. I got ready to endure due punishment. And then – nothing.

On he walked. This dear citizen didn't so much as look at me. Didn't turn his head. Not so much, I say, as a flick of the leg. On he walked. Meek as a lamb.

As I've said, this kind of thing happens. But there's no malice. Only simplicity of soul. Tread on someone, be trodden on by someone – just keep on walking. What does it matter?

And this dear man, I promise you, never so much as turned round.

I followed him a long time. I kept thinking he'd turn round and give me a stern look. No. He just walked on. He'd never noticed.

First published 1927

Born in Petersburg, Mikhail Mikhailovich Zoshchenko (1895-1958) attended school and university there. He served as an officer in the First World War but volunteered for the Red Army in 1918. He joined the literary grouping 'The Serapion Brothers' in 1921. His humorous sketches quickly became popular; 700,000 copies of Zoshchenko's books were sold in 1926-27 alone. He also won the admiration of other writers – from Maksim Gorky to Osip Mandelstam. Zoshchenko wrote his finest, and sharpest, work in the 1920s, but he went on writing through the 1930s and early 1940s. In 1943, he published part of Before Sunrise, which can best be described as his attempt to psychoanalyse himself and discover the reason for his lifelong depression. In 1946 he was denounced as an 'enemy of Soviet literature' and expelled from the Writers' Union. After this he wrote little of value.

Behind his mask of semiliteracy, Zoshchenko is a sophisticated and self-conscious artist. A previous translator, Sidney Monas, has written, 'Zoshchenko uses careless language carefully. [The talk of his narrators is] a weird mixture of peasant idiom, misunderstood highfalutin phrases, rhetorical flourishes, explanatory asides that are anything but explanatory, repetitions, omissions, propaganda jargon absurdly adapted to homey usage, instructional pseudoscientific words, foreign phrases, and proverbial clichés joined to the latest party slogans.' [1]

The central criticism directed at Zoshchenko by the authorities was that at a time of epic achievements he wrote only of trivia. Voronsky, the editor of the influential journal Red Virgin Soil (Krasnaya Nov') wrote in 1922, in a review of Zoshchenko's first book: 'This is supposed to be Revolution? Here we get backyards, little crumbs and tiny anecdotes. But that which shook all of Russia from end to end, the loud rumble that was heard around the world ... where is the echo of all this?' [2] In reality, however – and this may be the true reason for Voronsky's indignation – Zoshchenko registered this echo precisely. His stories perfectly capture the texture of everyday life in Soviet Russia, what Sinyavsky called its 'outrageous small-mindedness'; [3] the bureaucracy; the shortage of everyday necessities and of living space; people's readiness to denounce one another almost at random.

NOTES

1. Zoshchenko, Scenes from the Bathhouse (Ann Arbor: Univ. of Michigan Press, 1961), pp. viii-ix.
2. Quoted by Cathy Popkin, The Pragmatics of Insignificance (Stanford: Stanford Univ. Press, 1993), p. 60.
3. Sinyavsky, Soviet Civilisation (New York: Arcade, 1990), p. 199.

Travels to the Metropolis: Cape Town, London, and J.M. Coetzee's *Youth*

KAI EASTON (RHODES)[1]

I. Introduction

As you can see from these two illustrations of J.M. Coetzee's *Youth*,[2] we are in the metropolis, in London's Trafalgar Square.[3] *How we get there* in this text is, however, a marginal note in the greater narrative that begins in one of Britain's former colonies, The Cape of Good Hope.

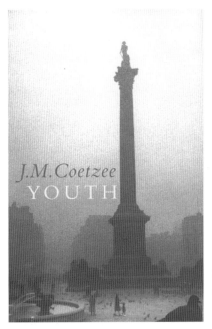 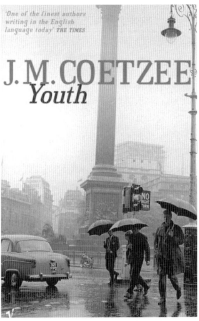

Indeed, this is a text that opens in Cape Town and forty pages later announces itself to be in England, in a bedsit in London's Belsize Park. Where is the obligatory description of the journey? Who is the protagonist and why has he left South Africa? Can we define this as 'travel', or should we speak in different terms about emigration or voluntary exile? (Remember bell hooks's warning that 'holding on to the concept of "travel" as we know it is a way to hold on to imperialism'[4] – we shall come back to this.)

In fact, the culture of travel itself figures little in this brief third-person narrative charting Coetzee's years in London after boyhood and undergraduate studies in Cape Town.[5] Leaving the former colony's 'mother city' in the early 1960s for one of the great literary centres, Coetzee undertakes a reverse colonial journey and one well travelled by emigrant writers, for example, Doris Lessing and Dan Jacobson. Coetzee's text, however, de-emphasizes the exterior journey and is replete with references to the voyage being one rather of 'testing' and 'transformation'. This is a narrator who talks about walking the 'cold', 'stony', 'labyrinthine' streets of London (Charing Cross, Tottenham Court Road, Goodge St), and who frequents not the tourist spots of the capital but bookstores, galleries, museums, the cinema. Compare this with his depiction of Cape Town: his reading of the colony, when he is physically on site, is of a landscape narrated entirely without glorification or detail – Table Mountain, against which nestles 'the university' where he is a student, is simply 'the mountain'; and while a few place names appear, there is nothing to act as a guide for those familiar or new to the landscape. Aside from what travel is required to get to home and back – his flat in Mowbray, work and studies at the campus in Rondebosch, Salt River Market, and a spontaneous expedition by foot with a friend (via Wynberg and Diep River) to St James on the peninsula – there is no other travel even within the Cape Province, except in a flashback to Worcester, which we have already read about in the earlier work, *Boyhood*.[6]

In *Writes of Passage*, the geographers Duncan and Gregory argue for the *physical* representation of travel, a reading and writing strategy which involves 'attending to the multiple sites at which travel writing takes place and hence to the spatiality of representation'.[7] Let's take my recent journey. Travelling from Cape Town to London today begins at Cape Town International Airport and ends, usually, at Heathrow some twelve hours later. But the more historical Cape Town-London axis is the route by ship, a journey of some three months from ports on the outskirts of the metropolis.[8] This means of transport has taken centuries worth of travellers, explorers, scientists, settlers, officials, artists, and missionaries to and from the Cape and England, including the narrator of *Youth*. And yet, it is exactly this physical passage that is submerged in *Youth*. There are but two references to the journey which, intriguingly, mention only his *arrival* at the Southampton docks (pp. 51, 165).

II. Reading the Colony/Reading the Metropolis[9]

If travel itself isn't the subject or genre of this book, the *reading* of travel narratives does indeed make a significant if only momentary appearance when, in the closing pages, we see the young Coetzee in the British Museum, allowing himself the 'luxury of dipping into books about the South Africa of the old days' (pp. 136-37). Sitting in the 'huge, cold city' of London (p. 57), writing a master's thesis on the celebrated half-English novelist Ford Madox Ford for the University of Cape Town [*in absentia*], here in the metropolis, in one of the world's best libraries, he is inspired by memoirs written by European travellers; in particular, he is nostalgic when he comes upon their descriptions of the Karoo. (We already know, from *Boyhood*, that the Karoo is where he most desires to belong.)

> It gives him an eerie feeling to sit in London reading about streets – Waalstraat, Buitengracht, Buitencingel – along which he alone, of all the people around him with their heads buried in their books, has walked. But even more than by accounts of old Cape Town is he captivated by stories of ventures into the interior, reconnaissances by ox-wagon into the desert of the Great Karoo, where a traveller could trek for days on end without clapping eyes on a living soul. Zwartberg, Leeuwrivier, Dwyka: it is his country, the country of his heart, that he is reading about.
>
> Patriotism: is that what is beginning to afflict him? Is he proving himself unable to live without a country? Having shaken the dust of the ugly new South Africa from his feet, is he yearning for the South Africa of the old days, when Eden was still possible? (p. 137)

Indeed, in the act of reading these historical travels *to* the Cape, the young Coetzee in London is 'brought home'. Does the fact that these writings reside in the metropolis and in the library of all libraries, the great old domed reading room of the British Museum, ironically authenticate his text of himself, his sense of place?[10] And do his own travels, far from transforming him into an Englishman as he hopes, merely confirm his colonial identity and his attachment to the landscape of his birth?

The extract quoted above is key to the argument I am making, for in this literary encounter we have a *conflation* of colony and metropolis, a reading transaction criss-crossing hemispheres. We must keep in mind that the colonial metropolis of 'Cape Town' is, in any case, intrinsically bound up with travel and settlement, from its beginnings as a refreshment station established by the Dutch East India Company (VOC) to its expansion into a capital city of one of the British Empire's key possessions after the Napoleonic Wars. This first 'foundational' history of Dutch settlement in 1652 – taught as *the* originary moment in most South African school textbooks until fairly recently[11] – is evoked in the following passage in *Youth*:

> What had seemed perfectly natural *while he still called that continent home* seems more and more preposterous from the perspective of Europe: that a handful of Hollanders should have waded ashore on Woodstock beach and claimed ownership of foreign territory they had never laid eyes on before; that their descendants should now regard that territory as theirs by birthright … Its orders were to dig a garden and grow spinach and onions for the East India fleet. Two acres, three acres, five acres at most: that was all that was needed. It was never intended that they should steal the best part of Africa. (p. 121; emphasis added)

But it is, after all, the *fact* of European imperialism that allows for the writings he is reading, and which brings him now to the crucial moment of imagining his first fiction – a travelogue of his own.

> The challenge he faces is a purely literary one: to write a book whose horizon of knowledge will be that of Burchell's time, the 1820s, yet whose response to the world around it will be alive in a way that Burchell, despite his energy and intelligence and curiosity and sang-froid, could not be *because he was an Englishman in a foreign country*, his mind half occupied with Pembrokeshire and the sisters he had left behind. (p. 138; emphasis added)

The present essay is part of an ongoing project which looks at Coetzee and Cape history. Although the 'Discourse of the Cape' which he speaks about in *White Writing* (1988)[12] is something I have been writing about for almost a decade now, my recent work is especially inspired by Coetzee's brief references in *Youth* to *Burchell's Travels*.[13] The title is the narrator's shorthand for *Travels in the Interior of Southern Africa* by the nineteenth-century traveller, botanist, artist and cartographer, William Burchell. Burchell's work, published in two successive volumes in 1822 and 1824, was compiled, after he left the Cape in 1815, from voluminous notes, sketches, engravings, a daily journal, and a most impressive and comprehensive map.[14]

We can see from Burchell's first page how his journal transplants itself (the diary entries of specific dates, for example) into his published record. Crucially, however, Burchell has edited, or omitted, any account of the journey from England. From the outset he places himself at the moment of *arrival* – his first view of the Cape. The first chapter signals its importance with the heading, 'Approach to, and arrival at, THE CAPE OF GOOD HOPE', and the first sentence reads as follows:

> At five in the afternoon (13th November, 1810) the sailors on deck, who had for some time been anxiously looking out, called to us that land was in sight.[15]

The immediacy of the Cape affects Burchell, and already on the second page we read how his *idea* of the Cape is altered by actual travel to the place, by the reality now before him.

> I now perceived that all the pictures which imagination previously forms of a country, make but faint impressions in comparison with those presented by the country itself …

Note in the following extract, too, that it is the *landscape* that Burchell focuses on mainly, a landscape which envelops the new metropolis, as we see in this description:

> As we passed along the western skirts of the town, I continued to admire the cleanness and good appearance of the houses, and the magnificence of the surrounding mountains. Owing to its great height and undivided form, *Table Mountain* does not at first appear to be so distant from the town as it really is; but as we approach, it seems to recede gradually, disclosing to the observer its enormous mass, and apparently, at every step, towering higher and higher.

Compared with *Burchell's Travels*, the prose in *Youth* is crisp, its purpose perhaps even one of anti-travel. For though London is the object of his voyage, it does not feature in any sense as a place that has truly been explored. (Or, thinking of it differently, has it in actual fact been explored to its depths? He walks the streets for hours on end, after all.) As for *getting there*, to come back to my opening remarks, we have only, at the end of Chapter 4, a sense of the narrator's great desire to escape South Africa after the events of Sharpeville, with the fear of military conscription on his mind and a growing detachment from the country at a time of raging Afrikaner nationalism. With political events taking over classroom time (he is in the middle of tutoring, but follows the crowd to the protest march down De Waal Drive), he leaves us with the words, '*Will the ships be sailing tomorrow? – that is his one thought. I must get out before it is too late!*' (p. 39). Thus it should perhaps not surprise us that he has fled country – but what about the voyage out?

Coetzee switches locations with Burchell more than a century later, travelling in fact to Burchell's home territory of London. Burchell himself is not trying to become a *colonial* (although he does push for and is influential in the 1819-1820 British emigration scheme to the Cape), but the young Coetzee *is* to some extent trying to 'become English' (p. 103). Though Burchell is an enlightened traveller and liberal for his time, he is indeed an expansionist. But he is also earnest about issues of representation, meticulous in his recording of what he sees. Nevertheless, the narrator of *Youth* recognizes at once a lack of *authenticity* in Burchell's historical account of the Cape and the Karoo, experiencing a sudden awareness of his difference from Burchell based on his cultural knowledge of 'home' and his embeddedness in this geography, even if it is, as he says earlier, 'on the shakiest of pretexts' (p. 17). While Burchell is admirable for his evocation of a landscape with which the young narrator is entirely familiar, his *foreignness* (compare Coetzee's own position in London) prevents him, it would seem, from being able truly to *imagine* it.

Until this moment, Coetzee's own reading and literary aspirations have been solely influenced by the great canonical writers, especially the late modernists. As Hermione Lee notes in her review of *Youth*: 'He is attracted to writers who have made themselves at home in England: Conrad, James, Pound, above all Eliot. The writers he most admires are all style and no confession, like Ford or Beckett.'[16] Beckett, of course, significantly comes into Coetzee's London experience too: it is on 'one of his expeditions to the city' (p. 155), now that he is working in Bracknell as a computer programmer, that he finds in a bookshop window a violet-coloured edition of Beckett's novel, *Watt*.[17] He instantly knows he has 'hit on something' (p. 155), and for those of us who know the story of Coetzee beyond *Youth*, he will be especially preoccupied with Beckett for the next several years.[18]

Most of *Youth* is an account of the narrator's attempts at Anglicanization or Europeanization, his desire to cut ties with nation and family, as we read in the passage below:

> Will his mother not understand that when he departed Cape Town he cut all bonds with the past? How can he make her accept that the process of turning himself into a different person that began when he was fifteen will be carried through remorselessly until all memory of the family and the country he left behind is extinguished? (p. 98).[19]

Indeed, *Youth* is certainly a book which could be read primarily as a story of modernist exile and alienation:[20] the young narrator wonders how one becomes like Henry James, a novelist who was able to 'rise above mere nationality' (p. 64); and he claims to want to leave his 'South African self behind' (p. 62). Though he does not warm to London or even England generally, he is devoted to the *idea* of it, as we are told first in *Boyhood*, by his childhood loyalty, by its opposition to Afrikanerdom, by his own English-speaking environment at home and at school; and, then in *Youth*, by a belief that only in the metropolis will he 'be transformed' and become a poet.

Throughout this text, however, there is a geographical and historical tension which interests me more. In addition to the bureaucratic inconveniences the narrator faces as an immigrant to England, bound by the terms of his work visa, and his choice of London over Paris and Vienna as a metropolis because he (a) speaks the language and (b) has legal access, we must register the current state of affairs in this particular relationship of colony and metropolis. Shortly after the narrator's arrival,

> with great show of self-righteousness, South Africa has declared itself a republic and promptly been expelled from the British Commonwealth. The message contained in that expulsion has been unmistakable. The British have had enough of the Boers and of Boer-led South Africa, a colony that has always been more trouble than it has been worth. They would be content if South Africa would quietly vanish over the horizon. (pp. 86–87)

At the same time, we recall the narrator's earlier claim that

> If a tidal wave were to sweep in from the Atlantic tomorrow and wash away the southern tip of the African continent, he will not shed a tear. He will be among the saved. (p. 62)

III. Travel, autobiography, and generic instability

South Africa under the Afrikaner Nationalist Party and their policy of apartheid thus asserts its independence from Britain just as decolonization is sweeping across the rest of the continent. But is the rupture between colony and metropolis really so complete? Can one just 'remove a country', as Coetzee's youthful paragraphs suggest?

The Cape of Good Hope has been a site of travel from Europe since the days, at least, of the Portuguese explorers in the fifteenth century. It has imported slaves, imported wives, taken in persecuted Huguenots and a diaspora of Eastern Europeans; and between 1620, when two commanders of English East India fleets first tried to claim it for the British Crown, and 1815 (when the Crown secured it), the Cape was tossed back and forth between two imperial powers (the Dutch and the British). What then does it mean to travel like Coetzee, the other way – *from* the Cape?

I promised to come back to bell hooks's cautionary question: does 'travel' carry with it the taint of imperialism? One might argue that Coetzee's seeming lack of interest in 'travel' as a subject in this book, in narrating in terms of travel, carries with it a subversion of conventions he has already (again subversively) used in his novels *Dusklands* (1974) and *Foe* (1986).[21]

But how should we in fact define 'travel'? Let's consider Iain Chambers, who distinguishes between 'travel' and 'migrancy' as follows:

> For to travel implies movement between fixed positions, a site of departure, a point of arrival, the knowledge of an itinerary. It also intimates an eventual return, a potential homecoming. Migrancy, on the contrary, involves a movement in which neither the points of departure nor those of arrival are immutable or certain. It calls for a dwelling in language, in histories, in identities that are constantly subject to mutation. Always in transit, the promise of a homecoming – completing the story, domesticating the detour – becomes an impossibility. History gives way to histories, as the West gives way to the world.[22]

If we go by the third-person narrator of *Youth*, Coetzee had no intention of either going to America or returning to South Africa. He does both. These 'facts' are outside the text, but do they change how we read it in terms of Chambers's distinction?

In closing, I wish to explore briefly how the *act* of travel and the *imagination* of travel that I have been focusing on might be linked with the instability of genre more generally, and autobiography more specifically. For if there is a crossing of cultures at work in terms of the generic ambiguity of *Youth* and its literary predecessors (for example, Tolstoy and Conrad, from whom Coetzee borrows his main title; Barthes and Henry Adams, from whom he borrows third-person narration and a rejection of traditional conventions of autobiography),[23] there is arguably also a series of *interconnections* and *overlappings* between colony and metropolis.

Borrowing from Frederick Cooper and Ann Laura Stoler's seminal Introduction in *Tensions of Empire*, and Catherine Hall's *Civilising Subjects*,[24] I want to extend our theorizing to consider not only the 'imperative of placing colony and metropole in one analytic frame',[25] but also how this idea might be related to what I am calling 'the contingencies of home'.[26] Certainly how we now think about colony and metropolis has become less oppositional, and their mutual influence and the dynamics of exchange have been elaborated on by many critics, especially Simon Gikandi in *Maps of Englishness* and Caren Kaplan in *Questions of Travel* (and remembering too Mary Louise Pratt's idea of 'transculturation' in *Imperial Eyes*).[27] But what if these very identities themselves are fractured and ambiguous before we even begin? What is the 'colony' for a young colonial, of Afrikaner stock, English-speaking but not English? What is metropolis to a young boy from Cape Town whose heart is in the Karoo? What is home? Without the ancestral link to Britain or the ideological or religious attachment to his Afrikaner heritage and the church, politics, and the community, how is he to be positioned? Why is he now in England in any case? Should he have gone to the Netherlands instead, or to Germany, in search of his roots? (Interestingly, the young narrator twice suggests he would likely be at home in Sweden because of his 'northern temperament'!). We might be better off considering James Clifford, who writes in *Routes*: 'Home is not, in any event, a site of immobility.'[28]

As for autobiography, so far I have addressed *Youth* as a fairly unproblematic memoir, in as much as I have alternated between referring to 'the young Coetzee' and 'the narrator', without yet questioning my decision to treat this book as tentatively 'autobiographical'. But the fact is, it is only paratextual material that allows us to do this so easily: interviews, especially from *Doubling the Point* (1992), the previous 'memoir' *Boyhood* (1997), and the marketing ploys of his publishers (sometimes referring to the work as 'fiction', sometimes as 'memoir'). One is also influenced by reviews. Perhaps the most interesting response – though not of course for reasons of authorial authority – has been from Coetzee himself. As Sheila Collingwood-Whittick notes:

> Introducing a reading from *Boyhood* during his stay at the Stanford Humanities Center in 1997, Coetzee recounted the question that had been put to him by his publisher about *Boyhood* 'Is this fiction or memoir?' to which the author had replied with his usual laconic evasiveness, 'Do I have to choose?'.[30]

Hermione Lee confidently concludes in her review that 'Certainly the facts of this life are Coetzee's'.[31] But if we go by Phillippe LeJeune's theory that the 'autobiographical pact' is based on the supposition that 'there is *identity of name* between the author (such as he figures, by his name, on the cover), the narrator of the story, and the character who is being talked about',[32] the evidence is fairly scant actually.[33]

On the other hand, genres, as Terry Threadgold has put it, are not static, they are 'processes, *poiesis*, not products, and constantly subject to change'.[34] And Laura Marcus has brilliantly argued in *Auto/biographical Discourses* that, if anything, the history of autobiography shows competing definitions, and a much more sophisticated interplay with other discourses. In other words, 'Autobiographical, authorial and literary spaces exist in complex interdependence with each other.'[35] This is nowhere more evident than in one of the many models for *Youth:*

Roland Barthes by Roland Barthes, which Marcus calls the renowned French critic's 'anti-autobiography'.[36] Coetzee's *Youth*, with its Conradian, Tolstoyian title, and its semi-present subtitle 'Scenes from Provincial Life II' that links it to *Boyhood*,[37] makes its claim to a European tradition, as Derek Attridge notes, 'even while it asserts its marginality'.[38]

Whether this marginality is *metropolitan*, or *colonial*, or *provincial*, depends very much on how we *read* these categories and, more importantly, the traffic between them. We might argue finally that *Youth's* ambivalent travels to and from metropolitan sites, texts, and genres is indeed a kind of *dwelling* (as Clifford would have it) which not only redefines 'the generic spaces of the literary',[39] but also challenges the fixity of much of our discursive/ geographical positioning.

NOTES

1. I am grateful to the Joint Research Committee, Rhodes University, for a travel grant that enabled me to present this paper at the 'Connecting Cultures' conference at the University of Kent in April 2004. Thanks also to Liz Gunner for inviting me subsequently to present it at the conference 'Imagining Texts: Media and Popular Literature in Africa', Centre for African Literary Studies, University of KwaZulu-Natal, September 2004.

2. J.M. Coetzee, *Youth* (London: Secker & Warburg, 2002). Further references are to this edition and are given in the text of the essay.

3. The illustrations are of the UK cloth (Secker & Warburg) and paper (Vintage) editions. The latter has embellished and coloured in the scene at Trafalgar Square, adding cars and pedestrians, black umbrellas and traffic lights. Significantly, this is the site of the South Africa High Commission in London.

4. Cited in Caren Kaplan, *Questions of Travel: Postmodern Discourses of Displacement* (Durham, NC and London: Duke University Press, 1996), p. 132.

5. I refer to the protagonist as 'Coetzee' somewhat too easily at present, but I will return to the question of authorship and the text's generic ambiguity in my closing argument.

6. J.M. Coetzee, *Boyhood* (London: Secker & Warburg, 1997).

7. James Duncan and Derek Gregory (eds), *Writes of Passage: Reading Travel Writing* (London and New York: Routledge, 1999), p. 3. True to my topic, this article has been written between hemispheres and metropolises, in my travels in South Africa between Grahamstown, Cape Town, and Pietermaritzburg, and in England between London, Brighton, and Canterbury!

8. Although steam-powered ships reduced the journey to 58 days. See Nigel Worden, Elizabeth van Hyningen, and Vivian Beckford-Smith, *Cape Town: The Making of a City* (Cape Town: David Phillip, 1998).

9. Despite frequent reference to 'colony' and 'metropolis' as if they were fixed and separate sites, the essay is actually playing with the idea of 'metropolis', using it in its more expansive sense, as in the following definitions given in the Oxford English Dictionary: '2. orig. Greek Hist. The mother city or parent state of a colony' and '3. a. The chief town or city of a country (occas. of a province or district), esp. the one

which is the seat of government; a capital. In extended use: any large, bustling city'.

10. Thanks to Kate Highman for articulating this for me in conversation.

11. See Leslie Witz, 'Beyond van Riebeeck', in *Senses of Culture: South African Cultural Studies*, ed. by Sarah Nuttall and Cheryl-Ann Michael (Cape Town: Oxford University Press Southern Africa, 2000, pp. 318-39.

12. See J.M. Coetzee, *White Writing: On the Culture of Letters in South Africa* (New Haven, Conn. and London: Yale University Press, 1988).

13. The first two essays in the trilogy are: 'Coetzee, the Cape and the Question of History', first presented at the ASA-UK conference in Birmingham (September 2002), and most recently in expanded form at the Wits Interdisciplinary Research Seminar (August 2004) at WISER, University of the Witwatersrand. The second is 'Coetzee's *Disgrace*: Byron in Italy and the Eastern Cape c. 1820', first presented at Nottingham Trent University's 'New South Africa' Colloquium (April 2003) and subsequently at the conference, 'The Eastern Cape: Historical Legacies and New Challenges' (Working Papers Series, no. 35: East London: Fort Hare Institute of Social and Economic Research, August 2003).

14. William Burchell, *Travels in the Interior of Southern Africa*. 2 vols. (London: Longman, Hurst, Rees, Orme & Brown, Paternoster Row, 1822 and 1824).

15. Burchell, *Travels in the Interior of Southern Africa*. Vol. 1 (1822), p. 1. The following two quotations are from the same text, pp. 2 and 14 respectively.

16. Hermione Lee, 'Uneasy Guest' [Review of J.M. Coetzee's *Youth*], *London Review of Books*, 11 July 2002, p. 15.

17. Samuel Beckett, *Watt* (Paris: Olympia Press, 1953).

18. Once he leaves England, and this is well beyond the pages of *Youth*, he writes a stylistic analysis of Beckett's English prose for his doctoral dissertation at the University of Texas at Austin.

19. Thus it is intriguing to read from Coetzee's brief 1993 essay 'Homage' where he speaks about this same period, and reveals retrospectively an interest in 'writing home'. When he left for London, he says, 'there was no South African writer, novelist or poet, to whom I as a young man could turn for a significant and vital lead in how to respond to, how to feel about, and therefore how to write about, my *homeland*'. J.M. Coetzee, 'Homage', *Threepenny Review* (Spring 1993), pp. 8-9 (p. 8). Emphasis added. As I have argued elsewhere, Coetzee's literary influences remain largely international and much of his fiction shares this internationalism; tellingly, however, his response to his 'homeland' has been in *provincial* – rather than *national* – terms. All of his works based on an assumed or identifiable South Africa are rooted in the Cape and Karoo. See, e.g., n. 13 above; for a fuller discussion of Coetzee and 'Cape Provincial', see T. K. N. Easton, 'Textuality and the Land: Reading "White Writing" and the Fiction of J.M. Coetzee' (unpublished doctoral thesis, University of London, SOAS, 2000). See also David Attwell, *J.M. Coetzee: South Africa and the Politics of Writing* (Berkeley, Calif.: University of California Press, 1992) who has highlighted Coetzee's regionalism.

20. Note Simon Gikandi's discussion of Graham Greene, *Journey without Maps*. He describes how 'Greene's African travelogue is generated by the idea of homelessness: to travel without maps is to reject the traditional notion of home as an absolute point of origin and meaning.' See Gikandi, *Maps of Englishness: Writing Identity in the Culture of Colonialism* (New York: Columbia University Press, 1996), p. 192.

21. J.M. Coetzee, *Dusklands* (Johannesburg: Ravan Press, 1974); *Foe* (London: Secker & Warburg, 1986).

22. Iain Chambers, *Migrancy, Culture, Identity* (London: Routledge, 1994), p. 5.

23. See Leo Tolstoy, *Childhood, Boyhood and Youth* [Everyman's Library, 13), trans. by C. J. Hogarth (London: David Campbell, 1991); Joseph Conrad, *Youth: A Narrative and Two Other Stories* [Collection of British Authors] (Leipzig: Bernhard Tauchnitz, 1927); Roland Barthes, *Roland Barthes by Roland Barthes*, trans. by Richard Howard (New York: Hill and Wang [Farrar, Strauss and Giroux, Inc.], 1977); and Henry Adams, *The Education of Henry Adams: An Autobiography* (Boston: Houghton Mifflin Company, 1961 [1918]). The influence of Barthes is especially striking. Throughout the text Barthes alternates between third-, second- and first-person narration, but his 'pre-text' in italics alerts us to Coetzee's project in *Boyhood* and *Youth*: that mingling with the story of "'family romance'" (in Barthes's case perhaps more than Coetzee's) are 'only the figurations of the body's prehistory – of that body making its way toward the labor and the pleasure of writing'.

24. See Frederick Cooper and Ann Laura Stoler (eds), *Tensions of Empire: Colonial Cultures in a Bourgeois World* (Berkeley, Calif.: University of California Press, 1997); Catherine Hall, *Civilising Subjects: Metropole and Colony in the English Imagination 1830-1867* (Cambridge: Polity Press, 2002).

25. Hall, *Civilising Subjects*, p. 9.

26. Compare 'the contingency of metropolitan-colonial connections', Cooper and Stoler, 'Introduction', *Tensions of Empire*, p. 1.

27. As quoted in Pratt's abstract: 'The concept of transculturation is used to introduce questions about the ways in which modes of representation from the metropolis are received and appropriated by groups on the periphery – and how transculturation from the colonies to the metropolis takes place.' Mary Louise Pratt, *Imperial Eyes: Travel Writing and Transculturation* (London and New York: Routledge, 1992).

28. James Clifford, *Routes: Travel and Translation in the Late Twentieth Century* (Cambridge, Mass. and London: Harvard University Press, 1997), p. 85.

29. On 'autrebiography', see J.M. Coetzee, *Doubling the Point: Essays and Interviews*, ed. by David Attwell (Cambridge, Mass. and London: Harvard University Press, 1992), p. 394; Derek Attridge, J.M. Coetzee's *Boyhood*, Confession and Truth', *Critical Survey* 11, 2 (1999), pp. 77-93; and Sheila Collingwood-Whittick, 'Autobiography as Autrebiography: The Fictionalisation of the Self in J.M. Coetzee's *Boyhood: Scenes from Provincial Life*', *Commonwealth Essays and Studies*, 24, 1 (Autumn 2001), pp. 13-23.

30. Collingwood-Whittick, 'Autobiography as *Autre*biography', p. 14.

31. Lee, 'Uneasy Guest', p. 14.

32. See Philippe Lejeune, 'The Autobiographical Pact', in *On Autobiography*, ed., Paul John Eakin, trans. by Katherine Leary (Minneapolis: University of Minnesota Press, 1989). Cited in (and translation modified by) Laura Marcus, *Auto/biographical Discourses: Theory-Criticism-Practice* (Manchester: Manchester University Press, 1994), p. 254.

33. E.g., we read his first name in the scolding letter from his cousin, addressed 'Beste John'; Professor Howarth is indeed the real John Coetzee's supervisor for his MA thesis on Ford at UCT. However, the surname 'Coetzee' is not once inserted into the text. As readers familiar with his work, we might find ourselves automatically linking *Youth* to the 'facts' of *Boyhood*, inserting it too into the 'memoir-novel' that began with *Dusklands* and that was also developed in his intellectual autobiography, *Doubling the Point*.

34. Terry Threadgold, *Feminist Poetics: Poiesis, Performance, Histories* (London and New York: Routledge, 1997), p. 97.

35. Marcus, *Auto/biographical Discourses*, p. 268.

36. As Marcus elaborates here (*Auto/biographical Discourses*, p. 268): 'Barthes repudiates the life-as-biography and refuses to be a party to the autobiographical pact: "It must all be considered as if spoken by a character in a novel" are the words that appear, in handwriting, on the page between the title-page and "the body of the text", the "signed" authorial directive (we assume) at odds with the fictional pact'. See also Linda Anderson's discussion of Barthes in *Autobiography* [The New Critical Idiom] (London and New York: Routledge, 2001), pp. 70-79.
37. It has echoes particularly of the British novelist William Cooper's *Scenes from Provincial Life: A Novel* (London: Macmillan, 1950), but also the subtitles of George Eliot's *Middlemarch: A Study of Provincial Life* (Edinburgh and London: William Blackwood and Sons, 1888 [1874]); and Gustav Flaubert's *Madame Bovary: Patterns of Provincial Life* [Everyman's Library, 140], trans. by Francis Steegmuller (New York: Alfred A. Knopf, Inc., 1993 [1856]). See also David Attwell's review, 'J.M. Coetzee's Unlikely Autobiography', *The Sunday Independent*, 2 November 1997, p. 23.
38. Attridge, 'J.M. Coetzee's *Boyhood*', p. 93, n. 18.
39. Marcus, *Auto/biographical Discourses*, p. 268.

Through the Net Curtains

ELIZABETH COOK

I am in Russia for the first time, trying to find my way; trying to distinguish between projection and discernment since, only when projection is identified for what it is, can discernment be real. I am reading *The Idiot* in which Prince Mishkin calls children 'little birds because there is nothing better than a bird in this world'. I think he is right and this leads me to wonder how it would be for a culture and language that placed birds at their centre.

Bird Tongue

Of one thing we can be sure: that *BIRD*
is at the heart of this language.
The letter *BIRD* signifies 'bird'
but *BIRD* as phoneme is an element of many
polysyllabic words (giving,
to the untrained mind, an irresisible
suggestion of birdsong). Long labour,
the discernment of pattern and rhyme,
allow us to assign meaning
to three hundred and eighty-five words
and a putative grasp of verb forms.
We can also surmise that birds (the creatures)
were greatly revered in this culture (viz. *I* in ours).
One unusually extensive fragment
contains eighty-three instances of *BIRD* on its own
and great clusters of the letter *BIRD* in phrases.
We think this a hymn or a recipe. The letters are well formed.
This fragment also uniquely contains
the single instance of the letter whose value
we as yet do not know. The letter is shaped
like the head of a spear, or a leaf that is cordate.

My efforts to make a beginning in the Russian language and the Cyrillic alphabet have led me to reflect on the shapes of certain letters – Ya (Я) and Ioo (Ю) in particular – and to wonder why particular combinations of sounds, some of which may be dipthongs, are perceived in another language to be single and in need of a form to represent them. And what are the conditions that press upon a shape to make it satisfactory as a letter? If we come from another culture are our associations informative or irrelevant?

Before I set off I had six lessons in Russian from a retired lecturer in Soviet Law. He is too reticent a man to have revealed much of his history to me, but when I told him that my primary motive for visiting Russia was to think more closely about Osip Mandelstam, he stood up, set his gaze on the middle distance, and recited the Stalin poem that cost Mandelstam his life.

I have visited Moscow, Voronezh, and St Petersburg. These days in Red Square there are Marx and Lenin lookalikes (or dressed-and-bearded-alikes) who, for a small sum, will pose with you for a photograph. Moscow's Mayakovsky Museum whose helter-skelter design attempts to mimic the experience of the avant garde, leads you to the exit by sewer pipes from which are spewed the detritus of history, including the recognizable skulls of Marx and Lenin and Stalin.

This is not the Russia that Mandelstam knew.

In St Petersburg I experience an almost paralysing sense of overwhelm. So vast, so much – so much history, so much splendour, so much suffering. I am afraid to venture into the Hermitage too soon knowing that if I do so I shall tramp around its endless rooms every day and neglect all else in the city. Never has a building been so misnamed, unless the naming was an arrogant joke. Before I visit the Hermitage once, I go twice to the wonderful Anna Akhmatova Museum at the Fontanka House off Liteny Prospekt. The flat where she lived for many years, both with and adjacent to the art historian Nikolay Punin. The kitchen contains the metal saucer-shaped radio which Stalin insisted every home contain to be tuned to his single station. In another room is a small silver Chinese dish – it looks like a little coal scuttle – which Akhmatova used as an ashtray. At a time when it was too dangerous to write down her poems (nothing more fragile, nothing more strong), when the mind was the only safe place for them, Akhmatova passed them on to the memory of a friend. Knowing that her flat was bugged and that any recitation would be overheard, she would write the words of *Requiem*, two lines at a time, on a cigarette paper and pass it silently to the friend. The friend would commit the lines to her memory and the paper would be burnt. The ashes fell into this little silver scuttle.

Isaiah Berlin famously recorded his meetings with Akhmatova: the time when she, tears of emotion pouring down her face, recited Byron to him in an incomprehensible English. Byron is more popular outside Britain than at home. May he actually be *better* in translation than in English? Few non-Russian readers really get Pushkin, I am told; Natasha, who speaks excellent English, spurns my preferred gift of *Keats* on the grounds that all English poetry sounds ugly to her. Ugly and thin.

How can we presume to understand the poems of a language other than our own? Mandelstam, Akhmatova, and Tsvetaeva have led me to want to learn Russian and I wonder what I have known of them in the translations I have read. Now, with my six-lessons-worth of Russian, I can even make an ungainly attempt at reading them out loud and am as clumsy as a watchmaker in boxing gloves. I have bought three tiny editions from a French-speaking *bouquiniste* in an underpass at Gastiny Dvor. It is good to carry poems in your pocket – you never know when you might need one – but better to carry them in your head, and best of all in your heart.

One of the attendants at the Akhmatova Museum speaks fluent French. Casual meetings have turned up more speakers of French than of English, though the nineteenth-century aristocracy for whom French was a first language emigrated or were killed. This woman, Elena, used to work as a translator in a car factory. At her retirement she moved from Moscow to Petersburg – 'plus spirituel' – and chose this museum for her retirement work. The museums are almost entirely womanned by retirees augmenting their pensions. Some, like Elena or a woman I met at the Mayakovsky Museum in Moscow, are immensely enthusiastic and knowledgeable; others sit in a bored stupor waiting for the days to go away.

In St Petersburg I have rented a flat. Helen Dunmore's *The Siege* has evoked the Blockade of Leningrad so closely I can almost smell it. Now, in this flat, I cannot help wondering how many people died here during those years; how many frozen bodies were once piled up in that frost-pitted courtyard, awaiting a time when there might be strength to carry them further or a thaw to make earth soft enough to accept them. On May 9th – Victory Day – children run up to war veterans and hand them small bunches of flowers – 'S dniom pabiedi', they say, 'For Victory Day'. Old soldiers, their chests bearing rows on rows of medals, are all victors today, with their bunches of tulips and daffodils. Real flowers, like the lilies of the valley I bought for the flat. The Children of the Blockade also walk in the Victory parade down Nevsky Prospekt. Some of them dance. I feel untried, like Edgar in *King Lear. We that are young/ Shall never see so much nor live so long.*

Later that evening Ludmila, who has spent the day showing me her city, invites me back to her flat a tram ride away from the end of the metro line – and then on to see the local firework celebrations which she says will be much better than the ones in the centre. I am exhausted. Nearly white nights, thin (often peach-coloured) net or no curtains have joined hands with my excitement at being at last in Russia and left me dizzy with sleeplessness. This is how a junior doctor must feel. Nor do I enjoy big crowds. The thought of making my way home on the last tram and the last metro with a huge and drunken crowd makes me nervous. But Ludmila has no time for such foolishness and marches me to where the firework display – the *salioot* will take place. The size of the crowd and the amount of alcohol around match my fears. Only the atmosphere doesn't. The fireworks are late in arriving and a good-natured chant of *salioot salioot salioot* has spread into a rhythmic roar by the time the first fire explodes in the sky and we are pacified into quiet. Then begins a series of ever louder sighs of incredulity that such pleasure should go on and on and get better each time. The sky a canopy in which bright parachutes of stars hang, then slowly fall and fade – like giant Portuguese men-of-war.

In the course of these gentle explosions we hear that the prime minister of Chechnya has been assassinated. I notice Venus still shining; the one steadfast bright star.

When I get back to my flat in Grivstova Ulitsa, it is one a.m. For the next half hour I scour the flat for any piece of dense fabric which I might drape over the windows of my room and secure them together with a mixture of paperclips and safety pins to produce a kind of darkness.

Shopping for myself with so little language is a challenge. Countries more experienced in capitalism make acquisition easy – supermarkets packed with goods you never knew you wanted till you saw them. Here you have to know what you want and ask for it. I feel like an infant and that only if I ask nicely will I be rewarded. Easier to buy things on street corners where people – usually old people – sell produce from their dachas or whatever patch of earth they have access to in the hope of supplementing their completely inadequate pensions. The bunches of herbs – dill, parsley, fennel – are carefully bound in green sewing thread, as was the bunch of lilies of the valley which now fill my room with their scent of elsewhere. Tonight I have come home with a pat of butter from nearby Finland and a litre jar of pomegranate juice from Azerbaizhan. The label, hung festively round the neck of the jar, says that the juice is beneficial in cases of radiation sickness.

Through such small pieces I try to find a way; it is so easy to get lost or to misunderstand completely.

JOHN PASS

The Sermon on the Mount

Be ye therefore perfect, even as your Father
which is in heaven is perfect. Matthew 5:48

The prophet came this way. Must have.
In pyjamas maybe on a June morning, a Sunday.

The men and women, friends and family,
slept on in the cool house in their temple
of talk past midnight in the press

of ideas and ideals against each other
and into their pillows. From the wine-glass littered rooms

and along the orchard's edge, over the sluices
and up through toadflax into sage brush and rabbit brush
came the prophet, head full of what to say, and

where to say it – came not so far as the slope where the name of the town
was spelled out in quartzite capitals, not so far as the one ponderosa pine
near the first peak, not so far as the eastern precipice. But far enough.
Below, the lake paid rapt attention to the sky. The prophet gathered

everything in wide embrace: multitudes
of bunch grass, cherry leaf. Quail and chicks in deep
shade under the trees. Tremors of light and breeze and water

performed their sun-up miracles. But only the words she had rehearsed
entranced her. Only imagining the grown-ups hanging
upon them. Those heady, exalted, propelling words

unsummoned by the breathless world, refused to come
all the way there and be spoken. In sudden awe
of unconsidered immensities, or at

the whim of wilful thought exhausted, wind-
shifted, unconsciously practical (as one avoids
scat on a path) she stepped around

and over where everything slips
against knowing, eases past and pushes
in a new heat and shimmer of essence towards this, us.

The Height of Folly

To have worked so hard at something wisteria
comes effortlessly into

and sets adrift in an off-hand fragrant gesture
of silvery mauve. To have clambered house-high
in soft air *against* disappearance. Holding to it. Knowingly.

The Last Caspian Tiger

ROBERT CHANDLER

For most of the last ten years, together with my wife and various colleagues, I have been translating the work of Andrey Platonov, whom most Russian writers today look on as their finest prose-writer of the last century. Although he was able to publish some of his work during his lifetime, much was published only posthumously. His brilliant unfinished novel *Happy Moscow* was published in Russia in 1991 – 40 years after his death – and an uncensored text of *Soul*, a short novel Platonov wrote after his visit to Central Asia in 1935, was first published only in 1999.

Early last year, shortly before Harvill published our translation of *Soul*, Hamid Ismailov, head of the BBC Central Asia Service, suggested I go with one of his producers to Karakalpakstan, the poorest and most remote part of Uzbekistan, to visit the area where the novel is set and make some radio programmes to be broadcast in Russian. I was surprised and moved by this proposal, all the more so because it was through a conversation about Platonov ten years ago that Hamid and I first became friends. During this chance meeting Hamid told me that after first reading *Soul*, he had felt depressed, thinking he no longer had anything to write about: everything there was to say about Central Asia, it seemed, had already been said by Platonov.

I felt not only pleased, but also anxious. Karakalpakstan is an ecological disaster area, with some of the world's highest rates of TB and several other diseases. The level of infant mortality is said to be 60 per 1000. All this is largely because of the drying up of the Aral Sea. Soviet planners decided that cotton – which requires a huge amount of water – should be Uzbekistan's main crop; thoughtlessly executed irrigation schemes quickly reduced what had once been one of the world's largest inland seas to a fifth of its former size. The remaining water is highly saline, and laced with pesticides and other chemicals. The climate has grown more extreme than ever, and there are terrible dust storms; toxic salts from the Aral Sea have been found as far away as India. And 'Resurrection Island' in the middle of the Aral Sea was the largest Soviet centre for research into biological weapons. Stores of anthrax and other toxins are said to be still there, inadequately buried.

Platonov describes a low-lying area not far from the Aral Sea as 'a land that is pale and salty, as if its tears have dried but its grief has not run its course'; he also calls it 'the hell of the whole earth'. These passages may seem like prophecy, but they are also clearly allusions to Dante's *Inferno*. *Soul* is open to many interpretations but it can probably best be read as a fable about a spiritual journey. The original title, *Dzhan*, is a Persian word meaning *dear life* or *soul*; Platonov uses this word to designate an imaginary nation composed of the exiles and outcasts of countless other nations. The novel begins with the hero, Nazar, being ordered to return from Moscow to his Central Asian homeland, to rescue the Dzhan and lead them from 'hell' to 'paradise'. Following, however briefly, in Nazar's footsteps seemed something not to be undertaken lightly. I also felt uneasy about the prospect of being yet another Westerner who pays a brief visit to the region, says how terrible everything is, shrugs his shoulders and walks away. Nevertheless, I went.

The places we visit differ from Platonov's descriptions, but the lives people lead often seem similar. This becomes most apparent during our trip to Moynak, once the main fishing port on the Aral Sea. As we drive there, through what was once the richly forested delta of the Amu-Darya river (the Persian name of this once great river, also known as the Oxus, means *Uncle Sea*), we see what look like large patches of snow; this is salt, leached from the subsoil by irrigation or deposited by salty rain. We stop by a bus stop; a white-bearded man, a few children and about a dozen women are waiting there. The women, like most women in Uzbekistan, are in brilliant colours; some of their dresses are floral, others are geometrically patterned. We introduce ourselves. Rosa, the producer I am travelling with, talks to a Kazakh woman; discovering they are from the same tribe and even the same clan, they kiss. Within a few minutes another ten women arrive. Each new arrival shakes hands with everyone present. They stand tall, they walk with more dignity than most people in England or America. I am impressed – in this apocalyptic landscape – by their apparent sense of self-worth. Not for the last time I remember Platonov's definition of soul or *dzhan* as 'the wealth of the poor'. Platonov, I should add, is the last writer who can be accused of romanticizing poverty. After the famine of 1921, he largely abandoned literature for five years, working instead in land reclamation, supervising the digging of wells and the draining of swampland.

The old man was once the chairman of the collective farm. I ask him about Stalin. He tells me what a great man Stalin was; men like him appear only once in a thousand years.

We drive through Moynak, leaving the town by a dirt road. After a mile or two, we see a group of a dozen navvies. They are working on the road, which is soon to be asphalted; gas is being drilled for. They live in a cabin brought here on a trailer. They work for twenty days, return for ten days to their home a few hundred miles away, then work another twenty days. Water and basic supplies are delivered twice a week; they cook for themselves. How they cope with the winter cold and summer temperatures of up to 50 degrees centigrade I cannot imagine. They offer us some flatbread. I break off a small piece; it is dry but tasty. In the evenings they play cards or tell stories; there is a sense of comradeship between them. They are glad to have work, however badly paid. Sometimes, however, their wages come several months late. Often arrears are paid only on the anniversary of the country's independence in September. We ask one man, 'What is the one thing in this country you would most like to see changed?' His modest wish is for his wages to be paid on time.

Learning that we would need another few hours, and a four-wheel-drive, to reach the receding shore of the Aral Sea, we turn round. A jeep is coming towards us. We stop to let it go by, then hoot. The jeep stops too. The two men and one woman, all of them Russians, are reptile specialists from the Academy of Sciences in Tashkent. They are researching how lizards and snakes are responding to ecological change. They are in good spirits; a month 'in the sands' seems to be their idea of happiness. Platonov, I think, would have felt at home with them. One of the men, Yury, has even read *Soul* and was moved by it. The woman, Emilia, has a small grey-green lizard in a cotton bag. She takes it out and holds it; it is about the length of her index finger. None of us say anything memorable, but I feel glad – glad to have met a reader of Platonov somewhere so remote, and glad that this reader should be an ecologist. Platonov himself, nearly 70 years ago, stated the principles of deep ecology clearly and boldly:

> The blackthorn is imbued with a scent, and the eyes of a tortoise with a thoughtfulness, that signify the great inner worth of their existence, a dignity complete in itself and needing no supplement from the soul of a human being. They might require a helping hand from Nazar, but they had no need whatsoever for superiority, condescension or pity.

And in an article published only recently, Platonov insists, contrary to socialist orthodoxy, that neither socialism nor technology can alter the fundamentally tragic nature of life:

> [Nature] is not great and is not abundant. Or her disposition is so severe that she has never yielded her greatness and her abundance to anyone. This is a good thing; otherwise ... we would long ago have got drunk on nature, we would have looted, squandered and devoured her to the bone. ... Ancient life on the 'surface' of nature was able to obtain what was essential to it from the waste products and excretions of elemental forces and substances. But today we get inside the world, and in return the world crushes us with an equivalent strength.

Soon after leaving the scientists, we come across eight men digging a trench, apparently in the middle of nowhere; there are small bushes every couple of yards, and patches of salt. They say they are excavating a sewage pipe; once there was a sanatorium here, on the shore of a sea now sixty miles distant.

One of these men, Ruslan, says he has lived in Sverdlovsk and Moscow but has come back to his birthplace because it is better than anywhere in the world. Like Nazar and many other of Platonov's heroes, he is an orphan. That, he explains, is why he has never been able to buy a cow and has to do work like this. As I listen, I think of a visit we paid the previous day to the local orphanage. Some of the children there truly had been orphaned; many, however, were 'social orphans', delivered there by a parent. Often a woman starting on a second marriage delivers the children from her first marriage to an orphanage; the average wage in Uzbekistan is only eight dollars a month – enough for just one large sack of flour – and, for that reason alone, the presence of children from a previous marriage can create tensions. Raida Radzhapovna, the director, said that the number of children in her care has doubled in the last five years, to nearly 500. She also said that many children, struggling to retain a belief in their mothers' love, try to blame *her* for removing them from their homes. Ruslan reminds me of these children; his love for his birthplace seems to be the crazed love of a child who has been abused and cannot admit to his feelings of outrage.

Back in Moynak, we visit the Aral Sea Museum, the most dilapidated museum I have ever seen. There are paintings of the Aral Sea, before and after. There is a stuffed vulture, its feathers falling out. We look at photographs of the town's former pride and joy: the fish-canning factory. Several captions contain references to 'The Factory Party Committee'. Someone has tried to delete the word 'Party' – as if the legacy of the Soviet Union could be erased by a stroke of the pen. A few days later we will encounter another similarly half-hearted attempt at erasure of the past. Decades ago, a bas-relief of Lenin's head was carved into the hillside opposite the road from Khiva to Bukhara. This has evidently proved difficult to get rid of; today Lenin is faint but still visible – a reminder of how little has changed in Uzbekistan. Most Uzbeks, in any case, are nostalgic for their Soviet past, a time when Uzbekistan was more prosperous.

An hour later we leave the museum, the day's only visitors. We go to the fish-canning factory. Formerly this employed 5000 workers; now there are 300, though it is hard to imagine – since the Aral Sea now contains no fish at all – how there can be work even for them. We speak briefly to some women leaving the factory; a supervisor interrupts and suggests we speak to the director. We are taken to Sergey Ivanovich's rather grand office. He outlines his plans. Apparently a brave new future, guaranteed not by Soviet idealism but by American dollars, will soon dawn for the factory. First, for a few months, fish is to be brought there from the Baltic – 3000 miles by train, then three hours by road. Then the factory will start canning a species of soft-shelled crab used in fish-farms as a food for expensive species of fish; the crabs are to be farmed in nearby lakes. Hardly a word he says seems plausible.

We return to our hotel in Nukus, the capital of Karakalpakstan, in the evening. Before going to bed, I reread a passage from the beginning of *Soul*:

Night was falling in the distance; shadow had already fallen on the low, dark land his mother had led him out of, and there was only white smoke rising from the yurts and dug-outs where he had lived until then. Nazar touched his legs and his body in bewilderment: did he exist now that no one remembered him or loved him? There was nothing for him to think now; it was as if he had lived thanks to the strength and desire of others, of people close to him, and now they had gone, and they had driven him away ... A wandering plant, the rough bush known as 'roll-over-fields' or 'tumbleweed', had curled up and was rolling along the sand without any wind, off on its way past. The bush was dusty and tired, almost dead from the labour of its own life and movement; it had no one, no family, no one close, and it was always moving away into the distance. Nazar touched it with the palm of his hand and said to it: 'I'll go with you, I feel sad on my own. You think things about me and I'll think things about you. I don't want to live with them, they told me not to – let *them* go and die!' And he shook his reed cane at his birthplace and at the mother who had forgotten him.

Two days later we visit another museum. There we see an exhibit still sadder than the stuffed vulture in Moynak. One display case contains a stuffed tiger. The very last Turan (or Caspian) tiger, he was shot in 1972 not far from Nukus. Who shot him and why, no one appears to know. He was young, not fully grown, and there is a look of surprise on his face. Once again I remember Platonov:

Humanity – if it is not ennobled by animals and plants – will perish, grow impoverished, fall into the rage of despair, alone in its loneliness.

The Journey to Basant

SHANAZ GULZAR

Sunday – 08 February 2004
Finally I make it to the airport. It's taken a serious amount of bartering even before I get to Pakistan.

Rosie needed pocket money and reassuring that the plane was not going to go into any tall buildings, my parents needed a LOT of reassuring that as a British Asian I wouldn't be ripped off or treated in an inappropriate manner. I've asked them to explain that one but no explanation has as yet been given, and there may never be any.

Eeky, that's short for Tarique, is also coming along to Pakistan, as part of the reassurance package for my parents. Needless to say, I've had to reassure him, too, that he will be okay. I'm getting very tired of reassurances.

We drive to the airport in the most amazing sunset – reds, pinks and purples, clear and warm. A foretaste perhaps of the light and atmosphere in Pakistan ...

Seat 41J, next to the oh-so-lovely loos ... it's going to be a long flight.

Monday – 09 February 2004
What a journey! We've finally arrived at the Elite Hotel, MM Alam Road, Gulberg District, Lahore.

Dad's friend comes to meet us at the airport in Islamabad, walking calmly through the barriers past the crowds to receive us with a massive hug. A very tall Anthony Quinn lookalike, Mama Sadiq has travelled and cooked many foreign dishes in many foreign lands. In England he got taught to make fish and chips.

Mama lives in Rawalpindi, his house – I'm sure it's been modelled after an old Bollywood set – is a maze of balconied rooms that all look down onto the inner, open-air courtyard, where the family gather and cook and eat. He has twenty-two rooms, three daughters and three sons. Four of the children are married, two of the married sons live with Mama, and the married daughters with their husbands and in-laws.

We are given a huge meal cooked by Mama that unfortunately we are too shattered by the flight to enjoy.

Mama owns and runs a corner shop. The shutters go up and down according to his whims and those of his very loyal young customers. Nome, the youngest and brightest of the sons, has the unenviable task of being at the beck and call of the shop. I begin to think 'open all hours' is not a Yorkshire phrase, but was adopted after it travelled to England with the good old Asian shopkeeper.

After we've feasted, Mama takes us to the Daewoo coach station. The roads are seriously flooded after an unexpected downpour which has lasted two days. And after a series of near fatal manoeuvres, we're on the coach, comfortably seated for the final part of our journey.

So far the trip has taken nine-and-a-half hours; this final part is another four-and-a-half.

I prepare to get bored as it is too dark and wet to see anything, and Eeky tries to sleep.

We stop over at what is the Pakistani equivalent of a service station. Like everything else in Pakistan it definitely has its distinctive style. Eeky and I stand looking at the wilderness we find ourselves in; it's like some godforsaken part of the world where there will never be light. It's an amazing feeling to be in the middle of nowhere in Pakistan, on our own, without an uncle, or cousin, or family friend to keep an eye on us. Let the adventures begin.

Driving into Lahore we can see the glittering lights on the waterways as the city prepares for Basant, the biggest kite festival in the country. We're met by Lou and Tim, the other two artists/ researchers who make up the team. They have arrived ahead of us and have garlands of flowers to greet us with. This is where it gets interesting. Tim has never met any of my family and neither has Lou. Between them they cook up the idea that, in the interest of decorum, Lou would always sit on one side of me and Eeky on the other. All this elaborate planning because Tim didn't want to upset my little brother by sitting next to me. I think that, on meeting Eeky, the daft plan went where it should have gone from the start – into the bin.

A mad hotel lobby conversation, then the hotel room. A relief. I'm too emotionally wired as I begin to realize that this is becoming more than a research trip or artistic project. I feel there are questions I want answered but I don't even know what those questions are. Putting aside the festival, why am I here? I had to fight to get here and to take on a lot of people's fears which have nothing to do with me. I don't feel Pakistani as I'm British and my Britishness is more evident when I'm travelling. But do I want to feel Pakistani? Eeky is suffering from culture shock and that boy is definitely a Brit abroad.

Tuesday – 10 February 2004
Lou is renamed Bori Gori by the locals, translated that means 'daft white woman', the expression is meant in a good-humoured way. Lou attracts the biggest crowds, she's the celebrity in our midst, the rest of us are not as interesting as the bori gori.

Shahi Kila or the Old Red Fort is the backdrop for the Badshai Mosque where we meet our guide Altaf. He's a well spoken man who thinks that we're a bunch of nutters, apart from my brother whom he's taken a shine to, as Eeky's the only one who isn't drawing, filming, or taking pictures.

Our day starts in Mochi Gate which is the main bazaar for kites and all things kite related. The whole of the area near the mosque and old Lahore is a series of bazaars; you can find a wedding bazaar that sells all things wedding related, jewelled lenghas, jewelled slippers and everything bridally. My favourite is the pots bazaar, row on row of shiny silvery pots, which seem to give off iridescent colours. The narrowness of the alleys forces you to look into the shops and see what they're selling. If you squint, you can block out the modern references and imagine the Mughal days when court ladies came shopping here for bargains or for that particular tailor who sewed clothes exactly how one wanted them.

Wednesday – 11 February 2004
It's becoming a trip of extremes. From descendants of Mogul princes to the workers of one of the poorest villages on the outskirts of Lahore, the 'other' suburbs. Mareedkay is where most of the kites are made that end up flying in the Lahori skies.

Our visit creates quite a stir. I'm growing used to this but only because Lou gets most of the attention.

The village is poor with alleys even narrower than Lahore's. The buildings are in a bad state of disrepair, and the shops aren't so glitsy. There seems to be huge numbers of kites and many ways of trans-porting them – on the head, on donkey, motorbike, bullock cart, and even a tractor trolley. It seems the villagers produce kites and nothing else. There is definitely an air of poverty, one that you can almost taste.

As part of our process of recording the preparations for Basant, we need to see and speak to the kite makers in their workshops. Up till this point it's been a man's world but, at one of the households we are invited into, we find the father ill and the mother and children at work. The family are open and hospitable, and we're not asked how the footage, photos, or drawings will be used. The mother is amused that anyone would want to film her. She sends her youngest son to get some soft drinks for us. These are probably quite expensive for her, and I feel even more privileged. Their workshop is their living room/bedroom, and we're probably sitting on their beds. It's a three-room flat that they rent, above a shop and other businesses.

On the way back to Lahore we spy some Dorr makers by the road side. Dorr is kite string, coated with a paste of crushed glass and pigment. It's strung taut between two trees, the thin lines resembling a loom. For protection, the workers' hands are wrapped in rags and, in the way they move up and down alongside the Dorr, there is a rhythm that reminds one of a very well rehearsed dance. Not once does the person who colours the string get entangled with the man who coats it with glass or the man who reels in the Dorr once it is dry. If the Dorr makers were craftsmen in England then their technique and manner of work would be said to be professional. Not once do they falter in their work – it is as if they are used to people pulling up in cars to draw them, take photos, and shoot films. We, too, have learned to function under the gaze of strangers and even the occasional watering buffalo. And always, it is Lou who is the centre of attention. I don't think it's just because she's white, more because of the respect that visual art seems to hold in Pakistan. It's almost on a level with poetry.

For me, this has been the most difficult day so far. I feel an affinity with the people of Mareedkay whose poverty reminds me of the living conditions in Mirpur where my parents came from. I see in the mother of the kite maker's family my mum who used to do piece work at home in England, and also my aunts in Pakistan who do hard manual labour in the fields and tend the livestock. While Tim and I are able to hide our feelings and distance ourselves through our means of recording and capturing images, Lou has to confront in more immediate ways the subjects of her drawings. The result is that she finds the lives she is engaging with painfully moving. On their part, the family enjoy looking through her sketchbook and discussing the drawings with her.

Occasionally they get me or Altaf to translate, but mostly they communicate through nods, vigorous shakes of the head, and gestures.

Thursday – 12 February 2004
This is becoming a trip of extremes and contrasts. The highlight today is a lavish wedding, a middle class affair with very polite guests and a racially mixed guest list. We had met the groom at the Pakistani consulate in Bradford when we were arranging our visas. When Tim and Lou bumped into him again at the airport, he invited us to his wedding.

From the wedding we go on to a Sufi shrine.

The shrine is mostly outdoors with a smoky and charged atmosphere. Lou and I are shown to the women's quarters, a fenced-off area, eight feet square, part of a two-storeyed building with a courtyard.

The Sufi performers (if I can call them that) begin their dance of worship with a slow turning and spiralling of their bodies. This is done to a steady drumbeat which, as the night progresses, gets faster and faster until all that can be seen of the dancers is a collection of whirling shapes.

The dervish-like state of the dancers is something that they don't easily relinquish; they slow down to allow themselves time to breath, then once more become whirling clouds of fabric and sand.

We leave at about midnight just as they are starting to warm up again. A long day ahead of us tomorrow, beginning with a talk at the Punjab House University in the morning, a private and exclusive establishment … should be interesting!

Friday – 13 February 2004
Multi-media and Pakistani art students are not too compatible at the moment. Lou and Tim both have very successful talks, the students engaging readily with them and their work. The students understand what they are doing since, different though their mediums are, they lend themselves to a traditional approach.

My work explores video and multi-media in theatre. I use computer and multi-media tools in my art. The students find it difficult to engage with the alien nature of my work (or that's what I think); they are very attentive but do not have many questions to ask. I would like to go back and set them a project using computer and multi-media tools to create interesting and imaginative solutions to a brief.

Pakistan does not have a very strong theatre tradition, compared to visual arts and poetry, two art forms associated with the elite. In Bangladesh and India, storytelling as a form of entertainment is part of the culture of the masses. Impromptu performances of oral narratives, dance, and song are an everyday occurrence, and a normal part of life. In Pakistan there is a real distance between the average person and any form of art. I know that, had I been born in Mirpur, I wouldn't have had the opportunity to become an artist. Or even to see a painting. My life would consist of looking after the farm and the family, being a wife and mother, and the last thing I would be bothering myself with are grand notions of cultural identity.

Thank goodness I was born in England and painted my first picture at nursery school.

This afternoon we visit the Gurdwara in Lahore. It's just outside the Shahi Kila by the Minare Pakistan side of the fort. Sahib Singh, the Giani, priest for the Gurdwara, is forty-six years old but looks and behaves as if years older. His simple life is ruled by the hours of prayer. He lives there all year and provides living quarters for any visiting Sikhs from India. He, like Altaf, seems to take a liking to Eeky, and explains the way of life of the temple in detail to him.

The Gurdwara feels like a haven after the madness of the streets of Lahore. Its colours — white and a decayed gold — contrast well with the redness of the Mughal fort. As I was filming upstairs, the sky slowly fills with kites, dancing and swaying in the wind. There doesn't seem to be the same feeling of expectancy here that there is elsewhere in Lahore. The kites fly but the people are oblivious.

As I watch, a kite is cut and starts drifting towards the courtyard, but there are no children waiting to fight over it and claim it as a prize. This kite will be left to decay and disappear peacefully.

Saturday – 14 February 2004
The beginning of Basant. First, a visit to the park for the Basant Mela, which looks to me like a smaller and Pakistani version of Bradford Mela. We are to meet up with the art students from the day before but do they turn up? No! I guess that, as in Bradford, serious art students here wouldn't be seen dead at a Mela.

Later there is the pleasure of lunching at the Dhaba with the Bolshoi Ballet, Tim having managed to attract the attention of their hosts while photographing by the roadside … only in Pakistan will you find someone pulling up in the car to ask who, what, and why, and then inviting you to lunch with the Bolshoi! Good food, amazing fruit cocktails, but a tame scene compared to what I've experienced so far. I need to get back to the kites and the stricken splendour of the Lahori streets.

It starts on a rooftop to the sound of Noor Jehan, Pakistan's queen of music and song. The sky is lit with searchlights and torches, and filled with kites, kites, kites, and more kites. The spectacle is tremendous. With our cameras, we follow the course of the kites, capturing the silhouettes of the flyers framed against an animated night sky. A fabulous feeling.

Too many kites are falling on the cables, and the electricity is turned off. We stay on the roofs, watching the skill of the kite flyers, the crazy rickshaws being driven in the dark, people partying and generally having a good time, a procession of some dignitary or other, lit with torches, winding and drumming its way through the narrow streets of old Lahore.

Our hosts are men, with the occasional woman stumbling up the stairs, only to stumble down again when she realizes her mistake. Occasionally a misguided but kind-hearted soul will give one of us a kite, only to see it bokated, cut, seconds later. Our complete lack of skill amuses and entertains them.

The experience has been fabulous; but five hours later, exhaustion creeps in. Lou is still going strong but, dizzy as I am, I cannot film another rooftop or kite. I want to save my energy for tomorrow, and the view from the minaret of the Wazir Khan mosque, one of the best views of Basant.

Sunday – 15 February 2004
Yesterday was about nocturnal kite skies. Today is about finding kite wars.

We are to meet Altaf outside Shahi Kila in the early afternoon, and are given a lift by a complete stranger in a white car who, after introducing himself as a businessman, invites us to his house for a meal; the people of Lahore are most hospitable and completely mad. At the Kila, there is a big crowd in front of the gates which are closed. A Basant function is in progress and some serious VIP's have been invited, so security is tight.

People aren't being allowed in or out of the fort or the mosque. Altaf who has somehow managed to get in waves to us. At that moment, the crowd surges forward and we are propelled towards the gates. The police respond quickly with their batons. Fortunately they choose to avoid hitting us and even to let us in, no doubt on account of foreigners such as Lou and Tim.

The view from the top of Wazir Khan mosque is breathtaking. No amount of film can capture the awesome sight of a sky filled with kites. Nonetheless, drawn by the shouts of 'bokata', and children running to retrieve the fallen victims, I film the journey of the kites from ground level to sky and back again. Quite dizzy with the effort and the excitement, I come close on a couple of occasions to falling from my precarious perch at the top of the mosque.

At the end of the afternoon and the end of the celebrations, we make our way down to the courtyard. Tim decides to go back up for a last minute image scout, while Lou, Eeky, and I stop to chat with a young woman about her plans to study in the UK. She is concerned that Tim may be in danger from the random rifle shooting (casualties occur every year); and decides to go and warn him. They make it down safely, just in time to run for cover, as a large burning lantern kite comes tumbling towards us. It would seem there is more danger from falling burning debris than gunshots. These kites are actually lanterns which are lit and let into the sky at the end of the celebrations, but what goes up must come down, and often on to unsuspecting earthbound folk.

Tuesday – 17 February 2004 Wednesday – 18 February 2004
A frantic scramble to get rail tickets to Rawalpindhi and then to get other means of transport to Harnow! We go via Mama's house which means a good meal and some rest. It is four hours by car to my parents village, Harnow, which is in the Mirpur district, the short cut taking a lot longer than anticipated. We cross the Jhelum river by the suspension bridge that until recently was a death trap. The landscape is amazing and, along the route, the difference in the architecture is immense. The closer we get to Mirpur, the more ornate and kitsch the buildings become. One village in particular, Dadyal, has more empty palatial homes than anywhere else in Pakistan. The owners are expats living in England, who feel the need to show off their wealth. Mostly the wealth is non-existent; all the savings have been sunk into creating a status symbol that's a complete lie. I hate this kind of falsity and, ironically, our family home is exactly one of these white elephants.

This is the shortest visit I've paid to my parent's village. Usually I end up ill, and this visit is no exception. In Lahore I survived on very little sleep and food. In Harnow, asthma and migraines set in. The stress of being somewhere that feels completely alien, where I'm expected to behave with unnatural restraint, always takes its toll. I'm not the traditional Pakistani woman. Sure, I'm not way out there, but I have to be able to say what I think and feel. And this is one place where I have to immediately put on an act. Lou is with us on this visit and even she is amazed at the difference between Lahore and Harnow. My family, especially my youngest aunt, make her feel very welcome. I think it is easier for them to be kind to an outsider than to members of their own family who have turned out so different.

The village is where I'm supposed to belong, yet it feels more like a prison. Here they survive in their own little world and what goes on outside doesn't affect them too much. They can't understand why anyone who is part of themselves and their blood would find it painful to be here. We are here because I want to make sure about my feelings about the place; I need to know what the effect would be for a short period of time and if it really is how I remember it. Time moves on everywhere, but here they're stuck in the 1950s and won't move on for a long time. I don't think I'm ever coming back, not even for a visit.

Thursday – 19 February 2004
We leave the village as soon as we can, taking the normal route back to Rawalpindhi. It is great seeing the Mangla Dam and driving over it; it is beautiful and dangerous at the same time. Mama's family is looking forward to having us for a couple of nights and there are plans to sightsee tomorrow.

Friday – 20 February 2004
Again only in Pakistan does one go sightseeing in the dark! Mama is insistent we see the Tarbella Dam on the outskirts of Rawalpindhi and Eeky wants to see the Shah Faisal mosque. So amid rows, and upset wives and sisters, we set off in two cars.

First stop, the mosque. For me, the Wazir Khan in Lahore was amazing on account of its age, its openness to all kinds of people, and the fact that it didn't resemble a corporate image of faith and religion.

The visit to the dam is hilarious, as nothing can be seen apart from a dark expanse of water; just the idea of sightseeing when no sights are visible makes the occasion memorable for me.

On our way back, we stop at the Nawaz Sharif park which also doesn't have many lights as most were taken down when Nawaz Sharif was removed from power. We stumble across a fairground in the park and decide to check out the dodgems. Two cars tamely going round in circles in what looks like a concrete prison, and being used, so it seems, for purposes best not discussed ...

Saturday – 21 February 2004
We're going home. Two weeks are enough and this has been an emotional rollercoaster. Again Mama ignores all the rules, walks us directly to the furthest departure point, and stays there, completely ignoring the guards who are pushing him back. We get through without any problems although I'm surprised at the tight security in the airport. Tags are attached at every point and our passports checked four times, a little over the top if you ask me.

The plane journey is mind numbingly boring and too long. Still, it gives me time to reflect on the trip and the different kinds of people and skills and attitudes we came across. Sometimes it was an experience of extremes which, at that point in time, only produced extreme reactions. If I look forward to the making of the film for the exhibition, it is partly because it will help me to understand better my response.

Wanted

KAREN KING-ARIBISALA

There is a wing in my throat. A wanting-wing of flight with a bone caught in it; the flesh stretched taut-tight over bone, so that it strangles utteranced hope of resurrection at Easter time, which is coming, but not for me. Guyana-schoolgirl-me-black – me in England with Easter time approaching in this school of girls, girls' school, girls. And me. Alone. At Easter time.

Megan speaks to me. She does not speak of Easter time approaching. Of how I, the only black girl in the school, will be left in the school alone at Easter. Megan tells me to watch what she does each Sunday after church.

When I begin to watch her, it is cold Winter. There is no Winter in Guyana. Only hot sunning heat and then the voice-loud rains, both speaking strong of promise of resurrection. No Winter. And I feel dead as dead Winter.

Sunday after church. And Megan collects the dishes of each girl in the dining-room. Her face is thoughtful smooth as she does this menial task to the surprise of the girls and the mistresses and even to me. And I follow her to the kitchen where she picks up pieces of bone and cleans them; scrapes off the chicken from the bones. The knife she uses is cutting sharp and it slices her hand and she puts the hand in her mouth and sucks at the blood. Then she continues to scrape the chicken from the bones. Certain bones.

I want to enter her mind and what she is doing. But I cannot, even as she washes the bones and dries them with a cloth and puts them in a box which clatters with the bones. Her collection of bones grows; has grown. But I have not grown in understanding of what she does; is doing.

It is the season of Spring now and the sun is warmer on my skin, but it is not the altogether enfolding embrace of the heat of Guyana which I long for. There is still a wing in my throat. A wanting-wing of flight with a bone caught in it. The bone does not resemble any of the bones in Megan's collection. My bone is an alone suffering tormented bone which wants resurrection; wants connection with my Guyana home. Especially at Easter time.

In Guyana Easter time, I could believe in an ascended Christ who promised to return; who said He had to go so that His Spirit could come again; and though I couldn't see Him, I would never be alone again. This is what I want. Want to believe in.

Megan this Sunday after church does not collect the dishes with the chicken bones. Does not enter the kitchen and scrape the chicken from the bones, or wash them or dry them or put them in her box. This Sunday, Megan says there is a shop in the village which is open and we should go to the shop. And when we get there, she buys a paintbox and she opens the lid and smiles at my delight in the rainbow colours all bright. She buys a paintbrush and tells me not to ask her anything about what she is doing; but to tell her how we celebrate Easter in Guyana.

'Why?'

'Just tell me how you celebrate Easter in Guyana.'

As we walk back to school on the grey cobbled streets of the village with people in their indoor silence, I tell her of the Georgetown Sea Wall which spans the coast to prevent the water from flooding the city, which it does at times.

'Easter, tell me what happens at Easter. I want to know.'

And I tell her of the day when all of Georgetown descends on the beach. Families and school parties and Church groups holding baskets of cassava pone, polourhi and banana bread and coconut bread and curry and roti. How they spread mats and cloths on the sand to sit on and put up umbrellas to cover them from the heat. And the man who has a bike with a big box of ice attached to the back surrounded by cups which clink and rattle against each other; and the containers he has filled with thick gooey syrups. He shouts as he rides his bike, 'Shave Ice! Shave Ice!'.

You stop him and wait for your turn to come, in the crowd of children jostling around him; and you get so excited you push past and say, 'Give me shave ice with red syrup.' Forgetting to say, 'please'. Those ahead of you smack you and you go to the end of the queue. Then you place your order again; and watch the Shave-Ice man take his metal scoop and swoosh shave swoosh shave the ice; zwoop, zwoop, just like the way Megan shaves the chicken from the chicken bones. And then the Shave-Ice man packs the shaved ice in a paper cup and asks if you're sure you want the red syrup and if you want some condensed milk poured on the top for ten cents extra? Alright, it is Easter. Christ has ascended, you can have some condensed milk for free, he says, this Shave-Ice man. He has a whistle hanging from a string round his neck and he shrills the whistle and rides along the beach, his armpits sweating and his face.

Then there is a kind of hush in the sky. With people thinking thinking thoughts; and some crossing themselves. It is a holy hot Sunday and fathers begin to rummage around in their picnic bundles; but not for food, not souse or black pudding or anything. No, the reason for the day is seen and felt in the air and in the sky which is breathing in gasps and expectation of what will happen. With the kites. The kites are box kites and kites of different sizes and shapes and colours. The kites in the sky make it a mosaic of colour and soon there is no sky; only colour ascending in Guyana at Easter time.

After I tell Megan about this, the bone in my throat grows tender and it touches the Guyana sky at Easter; and this bone does not now hurt me, constricting promise in my throat.

Megan and I have arrived at the school and she asks me if the colours in the Guyana sky at Easter remind me of anything here in England. She opens the paintbox and I see those very colours in the sky of the paintbox. I see those colours, I tell Megan, but I don't see anything else. Anything else which makes me know with a certainty that Christ has risen and will come again. That I will never be left alone again. Although to please her I wish I could say otherwise. For the Easter holidays are fast approaching and Megan can't take me home with her like she usually does because Megan is ill, and I will be left alone at school, with Easter Guyana thoughts alone for company.

The bone in my throat, the wanting bone, hurts me so that I cannot speak to Megan again that day. Easter day is fast approaching. They will all leave me alone in this school and Easter Day is approaching.

In the dorms I watch the girls pack their bags. And I wonder if Christ lied to me about the Second Coming. About never having to be all alone, ever. He said, 'Lo, I am with you to the end of the world.' Maybe He didn't mean it. Maybe He was speaking in parables. Maybe He thought I'd always live in Guyana and never come to a British boarding school. He said, 'To the end of the world. I will be with you to the end of the world.'

Megan finishes her packing quickly, saying she's got things to do in the common room and would I care to come and see? It's to do with her collection of bones, she says. 'I do not care to come,' I want to say. She's made me talk of Guyana at Easter time, made me think of it. She has made nonsense of every promise she's ever made to me. She promised to take me home at Easter. And she hasn't and she won't. So what if the doctor says she is very ill with that disease? I could have helped her. If I were really her best friend, like she says, then I could go home with her. What if she never comes back to school? Megan's gotten so weird since she heard about the disease. And long before Easter she scrapes off the chicken from the bones; cuts her hand; collects the chicken bones and buys paints. The only reason why she's got away with being so weird is that the mistresses were told about this mysterious disease she has. That's why she's got away with collecting chicken bones and they haven't said anything.

But I'm curious to see what Megan is going to do. More weirdness which will give me something to think about besides Guyana, when she and the rest of the girls leave for their homes tomorrow; more time to think about this curious disease which makes her look so pale and act so strange.

I go down the stairs to the common room and there is Megan with the bones; her collection of bones spread out on a paper, on a table. She has an engrossed look on her face and her curly hair is all tousled as if it doesn't matter if it's combed or not. She has the paintbox with all the colours of the rainbow in it and she's dipping a paintbrush in the paint; and she's doing it as if she's painting some kind of masterpiece or something. Something really important. She dips the paintbrush in a glass of water, then in red; paints a bone; puts it by the fire to dry and continues like this until each and every bone is painted a different colour. The colours of my Easter Guyana sky. And the bones look so pretty. And the bones are wishbones. And Megan says they are an Easter present; just for me.

'Just for me?'

'Just for you, my dear friend.'

'But, but how can I make a wish on my own? You need two people to break a wishbone.'

Megan says, 'Mum has promised that I can talk to you every day from hospital and, when we're on the phone, you can imagine I'm here because I really will be here even though I won't be … you see we can still be together and we can make wishes. I know you'll be missing Guyana at Easter and everything and …'

'I'll be missing you, Megan. And what if the operation doesn't work out … what if …?'

When we embrace and I say goodbye to Megan, I tell her that only one other person in my entire life has given me a gift like hers. That person said I'll never be alone and He meant it. I didn't know that He meant it until Megan gave me her gift of Easter wishbones with the colours like the kites rising and rising ...

The Convent

FROM THE FORTHCOMING NOVEL *DRAGONS IN THE WILDERNESS*

JEAN ARASANAYAGAM

Siegfried went on his way. Back to Germany. I would never see him again but he would write to me, send gifts of money. On one of the visits his daughter made to the island, he even sent me a transistor radio to fill my lonely hours. But she did not come to see me at the convent. It was her loyalty to her mother. I had bought packets of the best tea to be sent back as gifts to Siegfried and his wife, but she refused to take the package to Germany.

I can hear the crying of the babies as they lie in their cots waiting to be taken up and comforted. The bond between mother and child is lost at an early age. Some of the girls who come to give birth are from respectable families, respectable in that special sense of belonging to a middle class background where morality has a special social code. Bringing up a child by an unwed mother is considered a scandal and disgrace. There is no way out. The child is taken over by the nuns and the young women, their liaisons covered up in this way, go back to their parental homes and are married off in the conventional manner.

There are also the mothers who do not have the means to bring up their children, so the nuns tend and nurture them until the time arrives for them to be given out for adoption. Foreign couples come in cars and take the babies away in their carrycots and baby baskets. They will be taken away to Germany, Sweden, Denmark, England and brought up according to a different way of life. I have often seen these children once they are grown-up, brought back to the island by their foster parents, chattering away in a foreign tongue. They were taken away when they were so young that perhaps they never feel a sense of dislocation from a past they know nothing of. Perhaps one day, when they are old enough, they will begin to question their identity for they will feel themselves different. They will come back to discover lost roots, to find out who they really are. To search for their birth parents.

I have not been able to search out my father. He was dead by the time I reached England. My father had not been able to share his home with me but then wasn't he a homeless wanderer himself? A traveller. An explorer. Mapping out new territory, making of it a temporary base. As a result he did not realize the importance of a permanent home for Cathy and myself. Perhaps he allowed himself to be easy in his mind about the two of us, as children installed in a Christian home. He had his own memories of a Victorian childhood in England. Going to the village church and listening to the sermons within those icy stone-walled edifices, sermons on heaven and hell, fire and brimstone. The period of his life as a traveller may have been a paradise which he had longed for and gone in search of. His wanderings over the face of the earth made easy by the paths and routes taken by other colonial adventurers, officials, bureaucrats, soldiers, and merchants. In that great political caravanserai, we were, somewhere along that journey, the incidentals of its imperial bartering and trade.

Before he left Ceylon my father had put us in the charge of the catechist who used to visit our home. The catechist and his wife had great hopes that one day I would marry one of their sons. My father had provided for us with a lifelong annuity. We would not be left destitute. The catechist, who came into our lives and who had the sanction to take over responsibility from our father, was a convert from his own Buddhist religion. Like the rest of us, he too had been caught up in the high-tide of Methodist evangelism which swept over the Uva valley in the latter part of the nineteenth century. In 1890, Badulla, which was the principal station in Uva, was a separate circuit under the superintendency of an English missionary assisted by a Ceylonese minister. I recall that period of time, 1893 to 1906, and the missionaries from England who preached and proselytized with sincerity and zeal in the province. Yet how many of them, the ministers and their wives, would have known the pain and hurt of two little girls whose father had left them when he gave up his management of the tea estate at Passara? We were seen only as two souls to be saved.

Later on, we were admitted to the Girls' Home founded by the Methodist missionaries. We were boarders, without homes to go to during school vacations. Eurasians. The fathers, be they English, Scottish or Irish, went away. The mothers remained behind. Were they not thought to be capable of nurturing us, we who had sucked from their breasts? Why otherwise were we weaned from their warmth, their love, language, and religion? I had felt myself divided by the contradictions of my inheritance the moment I entered the Girls' Home and mingled with others like myself. Eurasians. Some of the mothers were Sinhala women from the village in the Uva Province. Others were of Indian origin.

The rule of patriarchy was so strong that the men, the planters whom these women had lain with, had not even allowed them to name their offspring. The names were taken from some other memory. From some other part of the world, from links and connections that formed an alternate cord. But the child had derived nourishment from the true mother and nothing could destroy that blood bond. Nothing, not even those alien names that sought to dislodge the true mother from the consciousness. Yet my father was also part of me and I would trace his passage through my life until the very end. We should have shared a home but finally he condemned himself to loneliness. I will never see his grave or tombstone. A tombstone with his name inscribed on it but nothing of his other life in a country which had given us life through his seed.

When he left us, I was so young. As I grew older, I began to read and study books which led me in my imagination along what could have been his itinerary. Names of places, significant as colonial landmarks, began to register themselves in my mind. Malaya was one such landmark on the imperial map. Rubber plantations. But how did he get there? After he left Colombo, his next destination would have been Penang. I knew that he must have travelled on one of those ships of the Orient Line, together with others who belonged to the empire and were voyaging to the Far East to seek their fortunes. I imagined my father on the ship, handsome, imposing, dressed for supper, wearing his evening jacket, the one he used to wear when he dined with the other planters on one of their social evenings. Perhaps he found a companion with whom he talked of his life in Ceylon and of his tea plantation in the Uva Province. Were the images of Cathy and myself and our mother already receding from his mind? As he smoked his cigars or his pipe, as he drank his wine or brandy or whisky, did he feel that it was now time to change roles – to talk at ease with his compatriots, waltz with European women in their elaborate evening gowns, stand on the deck with his arms around one of them, charting his new voyage?

The time would come when that journey came to an end and he would disembark, stop over at one of the hotels on the island of Penang and then begin the next lap of his travels. He would travel by train to a certain point, and then take boat and canoe up the river to reach the plantation. A man in a suit of white tussore, his solar helmet or topi, drifting along the river with the bamboo rafts passing by at their leisurely pace, the thick jungle on either side. His luggage unloaded at a little fishing village, he would ride in a bullock cart to reach the territory to be staked out. Thousands of acres of virgin land still to be surveyed and mapped. Did he recall the hills of Uva, the Namunukula range, the placid green paddy fields, and the forest abounded with game? Did he think of our home, now empty of us, his children, of his woman? Did the past, slowly, gradually, become hidden by the mists that swept over, miasmic, the wooded range of hills? Both he and my mother were buried in separate graves, in different countries. After leaving the estate in Passara, he never saw her again. He never sought her out again. Her voice forgotten, she became one of the silent women. Is it for me then to speak for her and all the others? Yes, I will give her a voice. A voice that is her inheritance, my personal inheritance, and that of the era to which she belonged.

GERALYN PINTO

Forever Baboo

In eighteen thirty-five they say,
Tom B. Macaulay had his way,
When after much deliberation,
He gave us Western education.

All native wit he laughed to scorn,
And from those jeers, a breed was born,
Whose mind was bleached to purest white,
No matter their skin was dark as night.

Most native ways were then taboo,
To this breed of Anglicized baboo,
Who gave their all to the British raj –
Their toil, their pride and their heritage.

What magical agent, you then may ask,
Did perform this wondrous whitening task?
What amazing feat of alchemy,
Bleached a people's mind and memory?

The answer is absurdly clear:
It's the books they made us hold so dear,
And their language that we learnt to praise,
While it coloured our minds and shaped our ways.

Now Gandhiji was frail, and yet,
On the raj he coaxed the sun to set,
He told the Englishman to pack,
His cigar, sceptre and Union Jack.

But English! It was left behind,
To hold us in colonies of the mind,
It muzzled our thoughts so that we may
See the world and ourselves the British way.

And all the while that we were free,
We were modern baboos, you and me,
Who viewed our land so fair and wide
And imagined England's countryside!

With Enid Blyton's kids we roamed
In far off lands we took for home,
Our shrubs we turned into Scottish heather,
And were suited 'n booted, no matter the weather.

But our leaders were far better than we,
And strove hard to transform our history.
Every garden they touched turned into a 'bagh',
Every road, long or short, was a 'path' or a 'marg'.

Well, the decades they went slowly past,
And the glow of the raj it faded at last,
And we had come into our own,
Indians – proud and strong and all freeborn.

We salute our leaders in their mission!
We're proud of their inverted vision,
To foreigners, though, it shan't make sense,
This national enigma in matters of tense.

For our national leaders (God bless their hearts!),
Have forward-looking backward thoughts,
The past is made present with a turn and a twist,
The future, they say, need hardly exist.

With patriotic fervour, wind and strife,
They hammer out our national life,
They've even invented an old tradition,
To embellish our golden yellow nation.

For we are bright yellow, our neighbours are green,
A scenic border threads in between,
We've toyed with the sun on either side,
To prove our worth and boost our pride.

It's worth the effort, you must agree,
It's the surest sign that we are free,
This casual dispensing of future days,
With alpha, beta, and gamma rays.

But sometime, somewhere down the line,
We've begun, I suppose, to fret and pine,
For though we are both proud and free,
We miss a sense of family.

Sure, John Bull was an older brother,
The Queen in her castle served as mother,
And Uncle Russ, though a bit of a bear,
We thrived upon his love and care,

To us it's still a mystery,
That Russ should now be history,
We think of him with a tear and a shrug,
And sigh for one long last bear hug.

To our east a dragon wags his tail,
He snoops about and drops a scale,
We know that dragon and his wiles,
And the burning breath behind his smiles.

But to our west, beyond the sea,
Looms the mighty statue of Liberty,
And in her shadow stands a man,
Who's loved by all as 'Uncle Sam'.

We thank our stars for Uncle Sam,
Who's bold as an eagle, and soft as a lamb,
Upon this distant shore he stands,
And stretches out his kindly hands.

And in his hands he holds a pack,
Of KFCs and one Big Mac,
And with his amazing, incredible rates,
To consumer heaven he opens the gates.

Now, Uncle Sam is tall and spare,
And in his ways both just and fair,
He's the family we've been looking for,
So tell me who could ask for more?

But just when you think we'd all be happy,
Out pops some scruffy Socialist chappie,
And hollers, 'Watch out! It's a carrot and stick!'
(*Oh, shut up you Markie, stop being my-o-pic!*)

But red-faced he blusters, 'What of WTO?'
'For Godsake, you Markie, let Sam run the show!
Now swill down your coke, and don't make a fuss.'
(*Can't think why poor Sam deserves all of us.*)

What if to our arms he offers a twist?
Or boxes a ear, or uses a fist?
'What do you mean, Markie, "It's only a trick",
Can GATT be a garrot, is Pepsi a stick?'

You know Uncle Sam cannot be a snoop,
To low, sneaky ways he never could stoop,
All he makes is a quiet request,
For a few stars and stripes on e-v-e-r-y vest.

'Cept for this odious Marxist chappie,
To 'blige Uncle Sam we'd all be happy,
We'll act together at his behest.
(*We can't have Sam losing interest.*)

Let's turn 'round now and say, 'Old Hat!
Bye Brits, Empire, and all that!'
We welcome Sam's democracy,
And hail the American century!

Notes

Baboo. The preferred spelling for the Indian clerk who worked for the British colonial government is 'babu'. However, 'baboo' has been employed here for humorous effect because it rhymes with 'taboo'.

Path. Pronounced phonetically as puth, the Hindi word for 'road'. Several state governments, city and municipal corporations in independent India renamed roads, gardens, public parks, squares, stations, and institutions, as also towns and cities, after Indian leaders and various icons of national life. This Indianization is satirically viewed as a futile attempt to rewrite history because the objective was to erase all memory of colonial rule. In the meantime, far more important measures for securing the welfare of people were relegated to the backburner.

Golden yellow nation. This is a reference to the saffronization of India by Hindu fundamentalists. They often trumped up the old orientalist invention of 'a golden age' of Vedic Hinduism, which, they claimed, was lost during a period of Islamic rule immediately prior to the British colonization of India.

Scenic border. A reference to the picturesque north Indian state of Kashmir that has become a site of bitter contention between India and Pakistan with cultural nationalist ideologues on both sides fanning the flames of hostility.

We've toyed with the sun on either side. India and Pakistan have aggravated the inflammatory condition of the subcontinent by entering into a nuclear arms race. The nuclear implosion in Pokharan in India was promptly responded to by the testing of nuclear devices in Pakistan. The 'sun' is taken as a symbol of nuclear energy.

Garrot. In imitation of Ogden Nash's habit of changing spelling outrageously for humorous effect!

TAJINDER SINGH HAYER

Egyptian Summer

Friday from a Luxor balcony

The swimming pool's blue kidney
is cupped by hotel gardens
– chlorinated oasis
to the guests who whoop, splash and,
prawn-pink by the waterside,
filter out the muezzin.
Waiters bring drinks to deckchairs
as prayer laps the hotel
like the Nile around islands.

I view pool and minaret:
their problematic closeness;
their problematic distance.

Trading talk through a market place

> *"Hey Muslim?"*

"No. Sikh"

> *"Hey Bin Laden!"*

"No. Sikh"

> *"Afghanistan?"*

"No. English"

> *"Hey Maharaja!"*

"No. English"

> *"Pakistan?"*

"No. Indian. From England"

> *"Hey India"*

"Parents from India. Born England."

> *"Amitab Bachan"*

> *"Michael Owen"*

> *"Hey. Buy"*

> *"Buy"*

> *"Buy"*

Shopping in Luxor

He's not a hunched Bedouin
with cracked skin and camel
but says he's been to Lancashire
and says he's called Bob
Lancashire Bob
but I'm wise to the ploys
because the Nile's fifty yards away
and I know trade made it
the artery of Egypt
so I'm all arms
and mock aggression
exaggerated gestures
to show I know the game
I'm no ignorant tourist
with a lonely planet guide
to everywhere
and an open wallet
bartering's supposed to flow
through my veins
and I know he's selling an idea
and that all tourists
invest in a share of the pyramids
buy up plots
of imaginary lands
with cameras that say

'I'll take this
and this
and this'
and make a palimpsest
of papyrus sheets
that come with certificates
of their authenticity
I know
but keep thinking
of the massacre
and what to buy
and our almost-Western dress
and the money between us
until I realize

it's blood I'm haggling over.

Writing Off-Centre: Establishing Commonwealth Literature in the UK

GAIL LOW

Postcolonial theory and criticism have been such a ubiquitous presence in diverse fields of academic study over the past two decades that it is sometimes difficult to remember what was in place before *Orientalism* initiated the methodological shift towards a more theorized cultural politics of imperialism and decolonization. Yet there was an important generation of literary critics who, while working predominantly within the assumptions, values, and precepts of an Arnoldian legacy of English Studies, argued for recognition and study of Anglophone writing from the British Commonwealth, and addressed the now familiar postcolonial concerns of, for example, identity, nation, language, and place. Among these early critical texts are Susan Howe's *Novels of Empire* (1949), John Matthews's *Tradition in Exile* (1962), A.L. McLeod's *The Commonwealth Pen* (1961), John Press's *Commonwealth Literature: Unity and Diversity in a Common Culture* (1965), Joseph Jones's *Terranglia* (1965), Ken Goodwin's *National Identity* (1970), William Walsh's *Commonwealth Literature* (1973), Bruce King's *Literatures of the World in English* (1974) and William New's *Among Worlds* (1975). Two other scholars who figure prominently in these inaugural decades were A. Norman Jeffares whose lectures, articles, and campaigns for funding contributed significantly to the promotion of the discipline in Britain, and Arthur Ravenscroft who edited *The Journal of Commonwealth Literature* for fourteen years.

This cohort of critics actively canvassed for the study of 'Commonwealth Literature' at a time which saw a proliferation of new writing from Australia, Canada, India, the Caribbean and Africa published, but there was little scholarly interest in most institutions of higher education. Looking over the archive of their writings, it is only fitting that one acknowledges their part in initiating debates about the relationship between literature, politics, and history; and, crucially, about the difficulties involved in reading texts from other cultures. Thus, writing in the closing years of the 1990s, we find Helen Tiffin, Leigh

Dale, and Shane Rowlands drawing attention to 'Commonwealth post-colonial critics' who wrote initially within a discipline deeply moulded by the assumptions, values, and precepts of English Studies but also staged a critical resistance to its Anglocentricism;[1] Bart Moore-Gilbert pleading for a recognition of overlapping concerns between postcolonial theory and some forms of Commonwealth literary studies, and arguing that 'quite different assumptions, objects of study and methods can exist within the same disciplinary rubric';[2] and John McLeod asserting that, despite their ideological conservatism, the early critics were 'instrumental' in clearing an institutional space for the study of Anglophone writing, thereby 'ensuring that these literatures were not a minor area of curiosity but a major field that merited serious attention'.[3] Yet, despite these acknowledgements, discussion of this period of literary history is all too fleeting. At best, it is viewed as an aberration in the evolutionary ascent of a critically sharper and more progressive postcoloniality, and, at worst, as a throwback to the past when the last bastion of colonialism lay squarely in the empire of literary studies. But the battles waged to admit Anglophone writing to the academy deserve serious attention, since skirmishes over the appellation 'Commonwealth Literature' show that contradictions, ambivalences, and resistance inhabit even this seemingly conservative ideological critical endeavour. In this essay, I offer a preliminary and eclectic stocktaking of the presence, in Britain in the two postwar decades, of Anglophone writing from the Commonwealth which enabled (and preceded) the creation of a new disciplinary area of study; I also address the 'discoursing' of a diverse and disparate body of writing into the subject of 'Commonwealth Literature' that occurred around the mid-1960s at a conference held at Leeds.

I have written elsewhere of the mixture of ideological, aesthetic, and commercial interests that prompted the dissemination and promotion of writing from former British colonies, particularly the Caribbean and West Africa.[4] What is worth stressing again is the noticeable growth in the volume of writing from abroad that is published in Britain, and the amount of commentary it provoked. Diana Athill's memoir of her time at André Deutsch attests both to the interest that greeted writers from former British colonies and to willingness to publish them. Educational presses, such as Longmans, Heinemann, and Oxford University Press, were quick to see that the mood of nationalism which attended political independence would generate an increasing demand for educational and literary material that was locally written and produced. As Athill remarks, 'it would not only be interesting to get in on the ground floor of publishing for and about Africa: it would also prove, in the long run, to be good business'.[5] Heinemann's *African Writers Series*, produced essentially for African school use in the 1960s, generated significant metropolitan interest in writing from Africa, and, arguably, the series for a time became synonymous with African writing. André Deutsch apart, other general publishers, like Faber and Faber, Michael Joseph, Martin Secker, Peter Owen, Hutchinson, also played a vital role in publishing writers from newly independent nations or soon-to-be independent colonies, and facilitated their entry into the cultural and symbolic circuit of the British literary establishment. Authors such as Patrick White, Judith Wright, Amos Tutuola, Wole Soyinka, Chinua Achebe, Ngugi wa Thiong'o, Nadine Gordimer, Doris Lessing, Peter Abrahams, R.K. Narayan, and Anita Desai were just a few of the names from outside Europe and America who made their reputations during the 1950s and 1960s. The arrival of Caribbean novelists and poets in Britain such as Sam Selvon, George Lamming, Edgar Mittelholzer, Michael Anthony, V.S. Naipaul, Wilson Harris and Edward Brathwaite, and the network of literary relationships forged in London, made their presence felt all the more. As early as 1952, Arthur Calder Marshall was to predict that the emergence of a new generation of West Indian and African writers would bring 'fresh and vital qualities' to English literature in English.[6]

Marshall's remarks are echoed down the decade; many commentators make the observation that something short of a revolution in literary terms was taking place within Anglophone writing. A steady stream of articles and reviews appeared which took as its subject writing in English from across the Commonwealth and beyond. *The Times Literary Supplement* (*TLS*), for example, ran a special issue in the autumn of 1952 entitled 'Fresh minds at work: Reflections on the Practice of Letters among the younger generation at home and overseas.'[7] Its special autumn supplement in 1955 focused on the impossibly grand literary theme of 'Writing Abroad', and devoted substantial sections to Australia, Canada, the Caribbean, Africa, India and Pakistan.[8] The critical discussion is both serious and illuminating, addressing the difficulties of local publishing, the themes of literary exile, landscape and national identity, and the distinctiveness of the individual works of fiction and poetry. John Lehmann's *London Magazine* had proclaimed in his inaugural foreword of 1954 that the journal would showcase international literary excellence from not only Europe and the United States, but 'from the English-speaking countries that are our fellow members in the Queen's Commonwealth'.[9] A special issue on South African writing appeared in 1957, prefaced with the somewhat partonizing assertion that 'what is being written in many of the overseas countries of the British Commonwealth now stands entirely on its own legs'.[10] An influential postwar literary and critical magazine, *London Magazine* continued, under the editorship of Alan Ross from 1961, to publish international writing and to review writing from various parts of the globe. Derek Walcott, Nadine Gordimer, Doris Lessing, Christopher Hope were some of the familiar names to appear in its pages.

That the new writing amounted to a tour de force is generally acknowledged in literary reviews and supplements. Francis Wyndham, writing in *The Spectator* in 1958, asks if something needs to be made of the fact that 'many of the most interesting postwar French books are by North Africans, while in the English literary scene of the fifties West Indian writers play an increasingly prominent part?'[11] In 1962, the *TLS*'s 'special number' on 'A Language in Common' proclaims that 'outside England and the United States a literature is shooting up, extraordinarily full of life', with 'fresh scenes, fresh outlooks and ideas which differ as sharply from one another as do their countries of origin'.[12] These literatures, the editorial goes on to observe, would enrich not only English literature, but also the literary use to which the English language is put, stretching 'the common tongue in a variety of new directions'. The proliferation of such writing from abroad is sure to offer a 'formidable challenge' to English writers, and the editor counsels greater awareness of the new literatures not only to counter English 'parochialism' and complacency but to 'give a new sense of direction to all who are concerned with experimental writing'. Contributors uphold the editorial line that the English themselves have no 'special proprietorial' rights to the language and the use it is put to. 'The Give-and-Take of English', one of the very first articles in the issue, situates the rise of Anglophone literature squarely within the legacy of Macaulay's infamous Minute on Indian Education. Yet it also notes that the familiarity and ease with which English is used by people to whom it is not the mother tongue would wrest the language away from its originary frameworks, establishing what would amount to new *national* literatures (albeit in the English language).[13] In a survey of writing from West Africa, another contributor observes that the relative underdevelopment of a West African 'academy of letters' has enabled a 'healthy irreverence' and a degree of linguistic experimentation; to

African writers, English is no longer foreign but 'a language which is theirs to use and which they are entitled to mould and pound and batter into any shape they please'.[14] Publishing is also a topic included in the special issue and 'Books for a Commonwealth' looks at the difficulties of publishing locally in countries with little technological expertise or economic or cultural support for a fledgling book industry.

What must be mentioned about these early reviews is a willingness to address Anglophone writing outside Europe and America at a time when academic institutions in the United Kingdom did not reflect a corresponding seriousness of intent. While it is still too soon to come to firm conclusions in my research, my sense is that the use of the term 'Commonwealth Literature' as such was not widespread and, if used, it designated the political alliances of the nations with which these writers are identified. 'Commonwealth', in other words, functions more descriptively as a geographical (and political) marker than a signifier of cultural and aesthetic unity. Lehmann, writing in 1957, is perhaps one startling exception in that he foreshadows the later attempts to establish literary kinship between diverse forms of Anglophone writing. In general, while the reviews of the middle and late 1950s might posit a relationship between English literature and literatures in English, the tendency to mould these texts and writers into the shape of 'Commonwealth Literature' was as yet not pronounced

Jessica Gardner has argued that *London Magazine*'s choice of title is strategic, signifying not only a cosmopolitan urban space but a capital that was formerly 'the centre of the British Empire'.[15] In the foreword of the January 1957 issue of the magazine, Lehmann makes a case for the common ancestry of *all* Anglophone writing in his employment of an arboreal metaphor:

> One can indeed go further, and prophesy that the next few decades will show an immensely varied tradition in literature that uses the English language, because of the rise of literatures with distinct flavours, even with idioms and word forms of their own, in the other English-speaking countries overseas; so that very soon the literature of this country will be merely the oldest branches of a tree that has other strong branches, not only in America but in all the countries associated with us in the Commonwealth as well.[16]

It is interesting to note that, in this defence of the international remit of the magazine, Lehmann is willing to concede that the literature of the British Isles may simply be another branch of the tree of English (albeit its oldest). This concession disappears from later descriptions of Commonwealth Literature. Norman Jeffares's paper, 'The expanding frontiers of English Literature', is one of the first British interventions aimed at encouraging the 'serious study of Commonwealth Literature', and recognition of the literary excellence of 'other literatures written in English'.[17] In this paper, Jeffares picks up on Lehmann's metaphor and alters it at the same time:

> No attempt has yet been made to set up any serious study of Commonwealth Literature in this country, yet England is a logical centre for such work. She is the root of this tree of literature; her language runs through all its ramifications. Her literature, just as that of Greece was inescapable for the Romans, is something which writers in the Commonwealth and the United States cannot easily avoid whether they make the choice of using, abusing, ignoring or adapting this legacy. ... The language provides the literature, the flowering of the scholarship which preserves and protects the literature is its literary criticism. ... The study of literature is inclusive. It would be more than churlish to avoid recognising the spreading and burgeoning of the parent stock, it would be stupid. English literature itself can be the more deeply appreciated if its ancillary and contemporary literatures are taken seriously in their own right, as part and parcel of cultures and civilisations which, while they sprang from and continue English ways of living, are developing in different ways, through accidents of geography or politics, or racial blending, or social philosophies.

Jeffares's emphasis on literary and cultural traditions (a legacy of colonial education and socialization), as opposed to Lehmann's emphasis on language use, results in the primacy of English as 'parent stock' from which other 'ancillary and contemporary literatures' spring and 'continue'. His allusion to the classical world lends British colonialism an added layer of symbolism. In memos and promotional literature directed at several grant awarding bodies to fund the activities aimed at furthering the study of Commonwealth Literature, Jeffares pursues this symbolism, describing English literature variously as the roots or the trunk of a great literary tradition nurtured by British soil.[18]

The Leeds Conference of September 1964, entitled (provocatively, it may seem to us today) 'Commonwealth Literature: Unity and Diversity in a Common Culture', has been rightly heralded as one of the key moments in the establishment of the teaching of Commonwealth Literatures in the UK. It was certainly instrumental in setting in motion the steering committee chaired by Jeffares that founded the present Association for Commonwealth Literary and Language Studies (ACLALS) in 1965. The conference also provided the impetus for setting up working parties on English language teaching, translation problems in Commonwealth literature, the teaching of Commonwealth literature, academic exchanges, journals and bibliographies in the field, and the subsequent commission on library holdings of Commonwealth literature in UK educational and cultural institutions. The reports of these working parties were published in the first ACLALS conference proceedings in Brisbane, although some general recommendations were published as an appendix to the Leeds conference proceedings.

The conference at Leeds must also be located within a whole hive of academic activity that was to lay the foundation not only for academic exchanges but also the ideological basis that enabled and created the rationale for such a subject area. In terms of institutional and academic history, one should not forget the cultural links that were forged between Britain and the newly independent colonies as the empire became dismantled, initially at least as part of a neo-colonial empire of educational aid and cultural studies. C.S. Leslie was to remark in *The Listener* in 1963 that a fuller understanding of the Commonwealth should be encouraged, for these 'resolute development and extension of the network of educational links, exchanges and assistance programmes … are part of the very fibre of the partnership'.[19] In 1964, there were five thousand students from Commonwealth countries studying at British universities, and John Chadwick estimates that ninety percent of these students came from the 'new' Commonwealth. Despite their importance, the ideological and political affiliations which were formed in this area of literary studies have not excited much academic scholarship. One can think, for example, of the specific contributions that institutions like the University College Ibadan (1948), and the various island locations of the University of West Indies (1947), made as external colleges of the University of London in fostering the movement of writers and intellectuals, and encouraging new writings in English.

While the Leeds conference of 1964 is often flagged up in the literary history of Commonwealth literature, some other earlier initiatives need to be mentioned also. The African literature conferences in the spring of 1963 were instrumental in signalling the growing importance of literatures from outside Britain, the US, and the old Dominions for the academy. John Spencer, then working at Leeds, attended the Freetown conference and wrote to Jeffares, enclosing a list of conference proposals. They advocated the inclusion of African writing in the literature curriculum of African universities, and academic research in, and study of, local literary and cultural activities. They also advised the quick establishment of an Association for African Literature in English that would produce regular bulletins to inform members of new creative writing and developments in the field. In July 1963, Jeffares hosted a conference on academic interchanges and research within the Commonwealth that discussed ways of improving comparative research and the movement of academic staff across different countries. It suggested a conference to discuss the topic of Commonwealth literature.[20] Later the same month, the Institute of Commonwealth Studies in London initiated a conference which attempted to carve out Commonwealth Studies as a distinct area of study. Kenneth Robinson's paper, which highlighted the difficulties of agreeing a definition of the term Commonwealth, argues that it should be taken not so much as a geographical expression as a political unity.[21] This desire to render a colonial and historical legacy as a political unity was already reflected in earlier, more pragmatic, British Council sponsored conferences on the teaching of English overseas. Its first Commonwealth Education Conference in Oxford (1959) proposed the setting up of staff and student exchanges, Commonwealth scholarships and fellowships, and recommended that the teaching of English overseas be addressed seriously. The second Commonwealth Educational Conference held in Delhi (1962) resulted in the Aid to Commonwealth English Scheme (ACE), administered by the British Council which outlined a career service in teaching English in Commonwealth countries. These schemes were conceived within a notion of educational aid whose purpose was a 'fostering' of contact between 'opposite numbers in the fields of education, science and culture and in the professions'. The Makerere College Conference in Uganda in 1961 proposed that the demand for qualified teachers should be met initially with expatriate staff; more importantly, it also, as Frances Donaldson records, stressed 'the interrelationship between language and literature'.[22] The relationship between English language teaching and English literature was to give rise to a conflictual and contradictory map of relations wherein language teaching was conceived of in utilitarian terms while language as manifested through literary use is directed at more social and ideological enculturation. The Leeds conference should be situated in the political and cultural climate of Britain at the end of empire where sustaining old relationships necessitated the forging of new alliances. The conference report explicitly endorsed the Makerere conference findings, and Leeds was funded in part by contributions from the British Council, the Commonwealth Relations Office, and, among others, the BBC and the Congress for Cultural Freedom.

Before I turn my attention to how Commonwealth Literature was imagined, discoursed, and talked about at Leeds and its aftermath, a sideways glance at what was happening outside the UK will help to explain the transnational academic connections that informed the Leeds event. One has to look to the United States, Canada, and Australia. Both Alastair McLeod and Robert Robertson, in separate accounts, have made the point that courses in Commonwealth literature were being taught in the US in the 1950s; Bruce Sutherland and Joseph Jones taught courses in creative writing from the 'British Dominions and Colonies'. The 1958 MLA Conference had a section devoted to 'Aspects of British Commonwealth Literature' (the Canadian presence here being particularly strong); the divisional subgroup 'Conference on British Commonwealth Literature' came into existence. Shortly after, it was retitled 'World Literature Written in English outside the United States and Britain'. The Conference newsletter, started in 1962, became *World Literature Written in English* in 1966. In other words, the growth of Commonwealth literature was facilitated by the expansion of American literary studies. This is reflected also in Jeffares's memo in the summer of 1963, addressed to the Vice-Chancellor at Leeds, where he makes clear their complementary relationship.[23] But if the increasing importance of American literary studies strengthened the hand of those wishing to make the case for Commonwealth literature, the US was also seen as academic competitors in a growing educational marketplace. Memos arguing for the creation of a Chair in Commonwealth Literature exhibit an acute awareness not only of what is happening at other Universities in the UK but in the US.[24] The development of archival and library holdings at Leeds in some ways rivals the parallel development of holdings at the University of Texas at Austin.

On another axis, the development of Commonwealth Literary Studies was also a by-product of a growing concern with national literatures within the old white dominions. This was especially true of academic courses at university level in the 1950s and early 1960s, where most of what was offered in the category of 'Commonwealth' was Australian and Canadian literatures. Needless to say Australian and Canadian writers were more readily available in print at metropolitan universities. There were serious attempts to establish comparative study of the two literatures in the Dominions Project, which was set up by the Humanities Research Council of Canada in the 1950s. The comparative approach can be read as a prelude to the methodology implicit in early responses to Commonwealth literature. Russell McDougall and Gillian Whitlock note that Jeffares, who was then Jury Professor at the

University of Adelaide, persuaded Brian Elliott to visit Canada in 1952 'to acquire a comparative knowledge of Canadian literature', and to see if an Australian council could not be set up along the lines of the Canadian Humanities Research Council.[25] Elliott's research interests were in Australian literature; he had already proposed an interdisciplinary institute of Australian Studies at the University of Adelaide which had not been accepted. After to his Canadian trip, he began to teach Canadian literature and argued forcefully for the formation of an Institute of Commonwealth Studies. But again, his proposal was unsuccessful, although the Australian Humanities Research Council was set up in 1956 through the combined efforts of Elliott and Jeffares and resulted in increased academic exchanges between these two countries. In 1957, Jeffares left Adelaide to take up a Chair at Leeds. He secured British Council funding to enable Commonwealth scholars to come to Leeds to do research and offer postgraduate courses. Leeds, however, was not the first centre for Commonwealth literature, that distinction belongs to the Institute of Comparative and Commonwealth Studies at Queen's University, Ontario, established by the Australian academic and critic, J.P. Matthews. Finally, with the expanding interest in Commonwealth literature, Australian/Canadian comparative studies, as McDougall and Whitlock point out, became more generally 'diffused' into the broader Commonwealth context.

To return to my central thread, what is designated 'Commonwealth Literature' was not only a moveable feast at this juncture but attended with the political and cultural concerns of the end of empire. Jeffares's memo to the Vice-Chancellor of Leeds, Sir Roger Stevens, around the summer of 1963, defines the subject self-evidently as writing from outside the United Kingdom and excluding the United States of America. The document suggests the discipline may have political significance, and remarks that funding should be forthcoming from government sources like the Commonwealth Relations Office (CRO) and the British Council.[26] Stevens's letter to Sir Saville Garner at the CRO, making a case for a centre of excellence in Commonwealth literature at Leeds, also stresses the educational and political ends of such activity:

> Literature has a very vital role in shaping the future pattern of emergent countries, in Africa, in India and in Asia: the common source for their writings and those of the older Commonwealth countries is English Literature. There is, however, little common knowledge of what is being done throughout the Commonwealth, and Leeds, as the one centre in the United Kingdom which is developing these studies, has been asked to hold a conference of scholars and writers from Commonwealth

countries, and to organize a bibliographical project which would provide a unifying source of material. I am enclosing a summary of what is being done here, and what we would like to do in order to meet these requests, which, we believe, serve useful educational – and political ends.[27]

It can of course be argued that, in seeking funds from the CRO, emphasizing the political importance of these activities would be a logical move; equally, it can also be argued that the CRO, in providing support for the event at Leeds in the form of, say, travel grants, must have felt that such events did not contravene the organization's objectives.[28]

I want to concentrate now on how this new field was talked about, imagined, and discoursed upon. I want to look in particular at the proceedings of the first conference on Commonwealth literary studies at Leeds. In his keynote speech Jeffares inscribes the emerging literatures very firmly within the orbit and framework of the Commonwealth as a cultural and political entity. The commonality and connection between nations is not questioned: the goal of the conference was 'wider and deeper general understanding and appreciation of … Commonwealth literatures, and what they have contributed, and are contributing, to our common culture through their own unique conservation and creation of traditions, attitudes, and ideas'.[29] The commonness of culture, language and a shared heritage is a motif that recurs throughout Jeffares's speeches in the 1960s. What is also highly significant is their strenuous reinstatement of the importance of literature within the educational curriculum at different levels, at a time when the central place of the humanities was beginning to be eroded. Literature has a fundamental importance alongside politics, economics, science, and technology; it is also (more traditionally) the repository of dreams, desires, national, and regional consciousness. English is conceived of as a common language of communications, a means of transcending boundaries. Consequently, literature in English at its best is also supranational and cosmopolitan.

Jeffares recognizes however that the centrality of the English language and English Studies must be recreated, reimagined, and fostered in the aftermath of Empire. English is here seen not as the sole property of its nation, since there are different kinds of Englishes spoken and written in India, Africa, Australia, Asia. Yet standards ought be upheld – only the best should be praised. Indigenous writers should not be 'incomprehensible'; they should value 'overseas markets'. Paradoxically, in asserting the importance of English as a world language (and by extension the importance of Britain in the history of Anglophone writing), Jeffares also seems to suggest that the centrality of English is the by-product of other writings in English. For new literatures in English, as he sees them, not only make a distinctive contribution to 'our common heritage', they help to renew, and hence keep alive, the language. The inscription of English literature at the heart of a vast empire of literary studies is to be expected – Commonwealth literature exists because there is a shared tradition. As Jeffares puts it in a later speech to the Commonwealth Section of the Royal Society of Arts in 1968, the Leeds conference delegates have a 'shared knowledge of the writings of English ... authors. They had formed their taste and no doubt their English style upon the same models, relatively the same canon of great writing ...'[30]

To read the proceedings from this point in time is to be aware of the ambivalence that is sounded throughout the conference. On the one hand, there is its implicit colonial framework. The Report and Recommendations section confidently locates Commonwealth literature within the paradigm of what it calls the 'English literary tradition'; students should be encouraged, it goes on to say, 'to study the development of the local English literature by seminars, visits of authors, inclusion in syllabus, and other suitable means' and 'University departments of English should study both by linguistic and by literary methods the relations between English literature and indigenous literatures in other languages'.[31b] On the other, the published conference papers actually reflect a contradictory and conflicting relationship with English literature. In the first section on Literature and Environment, the question of inheritance or adaptation becomes a central issue. John Matthews on the symbolic use of landscape in Canadian literature speaks of a partnership with the 'inherited legacy of British or French traditions' but also, in metaphors reminiscent of Conrad, of how that legacy is used as a form of disavowal. At best such an act of disavowal is ambivalent and at worst ineffective: 'a house of inherited opinions and institutions and ways of thought – British or French – which could be used to protect against the howling anonymity and unknown emptiness of Canada'.[32] W.H. Pearson extends the analysis to New Zealand, and argues that developing an independent New Zealand literature is, for the white settlers, a process of learning 'to recognise themselves in the limitations of time and place', and to relate to Maori ways and culture. Such a coming to terms constitutes 'a recognition of truths about themselves, both pakeha and Maori'.[33] Brian Elliot's reading of Mrs Campbell Praed's work looks at the critical contradictions involved in reading a colonial writer, while D.E.S. Maxwell's reading of Chinua

Achebe and Randolph Stow begins an inversion of the traditional privileging of art over history by arguing for an understanding of writing that is a consequence of differing political and historical situations. The struggle over land and the 'symbolic meanings of possession, of title' becomes the space which bears the 'imprint of the past' upon the present, a personal as well as collective drama.[34] John Figueroa's fleeting survey of West Indian fiction also grapples with the question of how to place individual novels within a developing West Indian novelistic tradition. It addresses the question of hybridity by raising the question of whose tradition one is to invoke. Importantly, it also locates the question as a relational one that must be answered internally (the creation and consolidation of a West Indian aesthetics) as well as externally ('part of a tradition of English writing').[35] A.G. Stock's paper on 'Background Difficulties in the Teaching of Literature' is interesting because of its post-Robbins inflections on teaching, and its central awareness that knowledge – or what counts as knowledge – is produced within disciplinary rules and institutional borders. She makes a virtue of comparative goals – 'to think with an integrated mind' about different cultures that students might belong to – but is also acutely aware of the contradictions within the disciplinary situation of teaching English Studies abroad.[36] Balachandra Rajan's paper which closes this first section of the conference proceedings looks at the conflicting demands that face Indian writers in English but ends with the observation that 'the clash is not simply between East and West ... but between the mores of a pre-urban [Indian] civilisation and [an India] ... committed to drastic industrial growth'.[37]

If English literature is at times invoked as the matrix only to be in some senses displaced, John Spencer's contributions to the section on Language and Culture makes a strong case for abandoning New Criticism's dogma of the autonomy of art. In many ways, Spencer's paper looks forward to the crisis of English studies in the 1980s and the erosion of disciplinary boundaries:

> But whatever solutions are found will affect English literature, and its teaching, and this makes me feel that we cannot expect the study of that literature, here in Britain as well as overseas, to remain as self-contained a discipline as in some quarters it is claimed should be. It must, especially when relating to these complex societies, have an historical dimension, a sociological dimension and a linguistic dimension as well as a critical dimension. ...The interaction of language upon language, culture upon culture, literature upon literature. ... [t]his perhaps calls for a new conception of the university department of English. It certainly calls for a new view of English studies.[38]

Many of the papers in the collection are acutely aware of the impact of place and culture on English (and Englishness) as a disciplinary norm, and of nationalism on writers. There are, of course, papers which show a strong Anglocentric focus, for example, Edmund Blunden's endorsement of Henry Newbolt.[39] But there is also Chinua Achebe's much anthologized 'The Novelist as Teacher' which restates the centrality of literature in a manner that is more in keeping with the debates and conflicts foregrounded and examined in the papers mentioned previously. If his account of the writer seems somewhat conservative in today's terms, it is also an account of a writer whose autonomy is not compromised by being called to take strict political sides.

Looking to the report of the working party on the teaching of Commonwealth literature, published in the proceedings of the first ACLALS conference in Brisbane four years later, gives us a sense of how things have moved on. The problems and difficulties raised at the Leeds conference seem to have come home to roost. The question of the disciplinary boundaries and norms of English Studies look increasingly unstable and untenable. Three of the five main points and recommendations concern the ways by which the English mould is invoked. The report asserts that the 'study of Commonwealth literature brings to the fore one of the basic tensions in English teaching – the tension between the need to proceed from the basis of an organised study of an historical tradition and the need to proceed from a basis of the relevance of literature for the contemporary individual'. From this it observes that Commonwealth literature forces a 'reconsideration of traditional approaches to literature'.[40] While the report labelled Commonwealth literature a 'minor' literature which should not displace the 'main tradition of English Literature itself, a tradition which will presumably contain the greatest examples of writing in English', it also asserts, in a moment of self-reflexivity, 'we cannot be as sure as we once were of what makes a work of literature significant, and what areas of Commonwealth writing may have a value which can no longer be observed in the "ancients"'. Commonwealth literature may need to be available to students who only have a 'minimal interest in English'. Teaching Commonwealth literature also raises a number of problems, for example, 'the danger of trying to force the teaching of a Commonwealth literature into the traditional mould of English Literature'.[41]

Finally, I want to turn to Arthur Ravenscroft's early editorials in, and letters pertaining to, *The Journal of Commonwealth Literature* (*JCL*). A journal of the kind which would include critical articles and annual bibliographies of creative and critical writing was proposed by the 1964 Leeds Conference report. So, with the CRO subsidizing the cost for the first four years, *JCL* was published by Heinemann Educational Books. As Ravenscroft remarks in the twenty-first anniversary issue, it was a bold undertaking at a time when 'neither the term "Commonwealth Literature" nor its referent commanded much acknowledgement, or even recognition, in Britain'.[42] Yet his inaugural editorial of 1965 indicates a self-conscious awareness of how problematic the term 'Commonwealth Literature' becomes in delineating this new field of study; he refers to it – almost apologetically – as a 'convenient shorthand, which should on no account be construed as a perverse underwriting of any concept of a single, culturally homogeneous body of writings'.[43] He goes on to assert that writers like Achebe, White and Narayan cannot be dismissed as 'belonging to the mere provinces of English Literature'. His second editorial records objections by writers and critics to the term 'Commonwealth' in the journal's title, but defends the rationale behind the journal in terms of information dissemination, and the setting up of a context of academic exchange across nations within which the reception of different writings is not distorted by the demand for exoticism or quaintness. Interestingly, in this foreword, Ravenscroft raises the issue of value and judgement in a manner that goes beyond the usual discoursing on good art as a kind of literary transcendence or universalism; in his view, the 'second main purpose of this journal is to debate literary values, even try to discover what literary values should be applied in scrutinising the literature of any Commonwealth country'.[44] His question, 'how does one assess a new African novel when there is so much uncertainty about what African novels are, or what they are trying to do', opens up the possibility that these new literatures will unsettle the familiar assumptions of 'literariness', literary value, and criticism. The unpacking of hitherto categorical imperatives is evident in the early scepticism over what is exactly common about 'commonwealthness':

> superficial similarity in the Afro-Asian-Caribbean writers to what is often found in the literature of the ex-dominions is misleading, if from it we deduce an overall common quality which gives the writings in English from so many diverse people and places a sort of shared literary 'commonwealthness'.[45]

Ravenscroft's doubts surface very early in the enterprise; in a letter to

Neil Compton in 1965, he asserts that the arguments put forward to exclude South African writing from the domain of Commonwealth literature are absurd, and remarks that, despite his lack of enthusiasm for the nomenclature, the subject has the welcome effect of lessening British complacency and insularity.[46]

The Commonwealth Arts Festival of 1965 in London, Glasgow, Cardiff, and Liverpool opened a floodgate of articles on aspects of the Commonwealth. In debates appearing in *New Statesman, English*, and the *TLS*, and in the documentation and brochures that accompanied the organization and presentation of the events, the term 'Commonwealth Literature' became gradually consolidated. Yet, even here, notes of disquiet were sounded. Dan Jacobson remarks on the 'obscurity and implausibility which surrounds the whole notion of the Commonwealth' in *New Statesman* in 1965,[47] while the *TLS* commentator points out in mock exasperation:

> The number of those who actually understand what the Commonwealth is and how it works must be very small indeed, smaller probably than those who understand the doctrine of the Trinity; moreover, unlike the puzzles of theology, it is changing all the time. ... If such a Commonwealth is itself difficult to grasp ... what of the concept of Commonwealth Literature?[48]

A more extensive survey of such publications and reports than I have been able to cover within the confines of this essay, and a thorough examination of the material connections and ideological forces that shape its institutional development, are necessary in order to offer a clearer sense of how 'Commonwealth Literature' emerged in these two, and ensuing, decades. Yet, as I have sought to argue here, both as a subject and a term, 'Commonwealth Literature' cannot be taken for granted since, even in its inaugural moments, it was highly contested.

NOTES

The research for this paper was undertaken with the help of a grant from the British Academy and from the Leverhulme Foundation. My thanks to archivists at the University of Leeds and the National Library of Australia for their help in locating the papers of A. Norman Jeffares, ACLALS papers, and various documents pertaining to Commonwealth Literature in the School of English at Leeds University. I am also grateful to A. Norman Jeffares for agreeing to be interviewed – and for his generosity with information and books.

1. Alan Lawson, Alan Leigh Dale, Helen Tiffin, and Shane Rowlands (eds), *Post-Colonial Literatures in English: General, Theoretical and Comparative 1970-1993* (New York: G.K. Hall, 1997).
2. Bart Moore-Gilbert, *Postcolonial Theory* (London and New York: Verso, 1997), p. 169.

3. John McLeod, *Beginning Postcolonialism* (Manchester and New York: Manchester University Press, 2000), p. 16.
4. See Gail Low, 'Finding the Centre: Publishing Commonwealth Writing in London – The Case of Anglophone Caribbean Writing 1950-65', *The Journal of Commonwealth Literature,* 37:2 (2002) 21-38 and 'In pursuit of publishing: the case of Heinemann Educational and the African Writers' Series', *Wasafiri,* 37 (Winter 2002) 31-35.
5. Diana Athill, *stet* (London: Granta Books, 2000), p. 103.
6. Arthur Calder Marshall, 'West Indian Writers', *The Times Literary Supplement,* 23 May 1952, p. 348.
7. See 'Fresh Minds at Work', *TLS,* 29 August 1952.
8. See 'Special Autumn Number: Writing Abroad', *TLS,* 5 August 1955.
9. John Lehmann, 'Foreword', *London Magazine,* 1:1 (1954) 12.
10. John Lehmann, 'Foreword', *London Magazine,* 4:2 (1957) 9-11. Lehmann, it has to be said, was not entirely insensitive to the offence which his statement might cause.
11. Francis Wyndham, 'Ways of Sunlight', *The Spectator,* 28 February 1958, p. 273.
12. Unsigned editorial, 'In Common', 'Special Autumn Number: A Language in Common', *TLS,* 10 August 1962, p. 591.
13. Unsigned article, 'The Give-and-Take of English', ibid, p. 568.
14. Unsigned article, 'Writing in West Africa', ibid, p. 571.
15. Jessica Gardner, 'Where is the Post-Colonial London of the *London Magazine*?', *Kunapipi,* 21:2 (1999) 95.
16. 'Foreword', *London Magazine,* 4:1 (1957) 7.
17. A. Norman Jeffares, 'The expanding frontiers of English Literature', *University of Leeds Review,* 4 December 1957, pp. 361-67.
18. Jeffares's archive of papers is located at the National Library of Australia, Manuscript number: NLA MS4276.
19. Quoted in John Chadwick, *The Unofficial Commonwealth: The Story of the Commonwealth Foundation* (London: Allen and Unwin, 1980).
20. Handwritten memo: Conference on Commonwealth Academic Interchanges and Research NLA MS 4876, Box 27/80.
21. Kenneth Robinson, Paper on Comparative Commonwealth Studies, Institute of Commonwealth Studies Conference, 8-9 July 1963.
22. Frances Donaldson, *The British Council* (London: Jonathan Cape, 1984), p. 216.
23. Commonwealth Literature Conference A6 1963-74, Leeds University Archives; for a discussion of parallel and/or institution developments in Commonwealth literary studies in the UK and the US, see Tim Watson, 'The US Beginnings of Commonwealth Studies', *ARIEL,* 31:1&2 (2000) 51-72. See also A. Norman Jeffares's rejoinder, 'Elementary, My Dear Watson', *ARIEL,* 31:4 (2000) 139-47.
24. School of English Chair of Commonwealth Literature 1967-71 folder of documents, Leeds University Archives.
25. Russell McDougall and Gillian Whitlock, *Australian/Canadian Literatures in English: Comparative Perspectives* (London: Methuen, 1987), p. 7.
26. Undated memo to the Vice-Chancellor from the Chairman of the School of English: Commonwealth Literature in English, Commonwealth Literature Conference A6 1963-74, Leeds University Archives.
27. Letter to Sir Saville Garner, CRO 14/10/63 from Sir Roger Stevens (Vice-Chancellor, Leeds University), Commonwealth Literature Conference A6 1963-74, Leeds University Archives.
28. It is difficult to gauge whether the decision to request funding from the

Commonwealth Relations Office was an unusual or unique move in the sense that academic subjects were not ordinarily funded through governmental aid in a direct manner. What is significant is that the Commonwealth Relations Office did not dismiss these requests in a cursory way, but engaged in correspondence with their respondents at Leeds even when these bids were unsuccessful. In my interviews with Jeffares, he has consistently bemoaned the ascribing of political motivation where, in his view, there was none.

29. A. Norman Jeffares, 'Introduction', in John Press, *Commonwealth Literature: Unity and Diversity in a Common Culture* (London: Heinemann, 1965), p. xii.
30. A. Norman Jeffares, 'The study of Commonwealth writing', *Commonwealth Journal*, 1969, p. 74.
31. John Press, *Commonwealth Literature: Unity and Diversity in a Common Culture* (London: Heinemann, 1965), p. 213.
32. John Matthews, 'The Canadian Experience', in Press, *Commonwealth Literature*, p. 24.
33. W.H. Pearson, 'The Recognition of Reality', in Press, *Commonwealth Literature*, p. 47.
34. D.E.S. Maxwell, 'Landscape and Theme', in Press, *Commonwealth Literature*, pp. 82-9.
35. John J.M. Figueroa, 'Some Provisional Comments on West Indian Novels', in Press, *Commonwealth Literature*, p.94.
36. A.G. Stock, 'Background Difficulties in the Teaching of Literature', in Press, *Commonwealth Literature*, p. 103.
37. Balachandra Rajan, 'Identity and Nationality', in Press, *Commonwealth Literature*, p. 108.
38. John Spencer, 'One Strand in a Pattern', in Press, *Commonwealth Literature*, pp. 118-9.
39. Edmund Blunden, 'The Cultural Role of the University', in Press, *Commonwealth Literature*, pp. 184; 179.
40. Ken Goodwin (ed), *National Identity* (London: Heinemann, 1970), p. 203.
41. Ibid, p. 204.
42. Arthur Ravenscroft, 'The Origins', *JCL,* 21:1 (1986) 3.
43. Arthur Ravenscroft, 'Editorial', *JCL*, 1 (1965) p. v.
44. *JCL* 2 (1966) p. vi.
45. *JCL* 4 (1967) p. iv.
46. Arthur Ravenscroft to Neil Compton, 3 January 1965. Ravenscroft papers, Special Collections, Leeds University Library.
47. Dan Jacobson, 'Commonwealth Literature: Out of Empire', *New Statesman*, 29 January 1965, p. 153.
48. Unsigned article, 'Sounding the Sixties: The Commonwealth', *TLS*, 16 September 1965, p. 786.

Paul Sharrad
Albert Wendt and Pacific Literature: Circling the Void
ISBN: 0 7190 5942 9   hb   320pp   £40.00
Manchester University Press 2003

Paul Sharrad's *Readings in Pacific Literature* – a collection of essays by various authors – has for some time been a helpful guide to those interested in the writing of Oceania. It is fitting therefore that this critic should now guide readers into a comprehensive study of publications by Albert Wendt, whose status as poet, novelist, playwright, teacher, and critic has developed in close connection with the (post)independence growth of Pacific literatures. The emphases of the title are, therefore, appropriate, since so much of Wendt's productive, innovative career has been facilitated and encouraged in tandem with the general success of this phase of Pacific writing. The challenge in a book with so much to address is how to balance scholarship with biography, historical and political analysis with literary criticism.

Sharrad's style is accessible, his research thorough, and his assessments balanced. The plot summaries will be helpful to students, as will the detailed reference to the many essays published by Wendt, some of which are not easy to track down. The introduction acknowledges Wendt's international status, yet recognizes that his readership and primary support group have been Samoan. Setting Wendt's writing in the structure of fa'a Samoa (Samoan ways), his life in New Zealand and Fiji, brings a social and political edge to the readings that balances realism, fagogo, fable, fantasy and allegory.

The study contains detailed research on the early years of writing, a contextualizing of the conditions of production, discussion of the tremendous impact of *Sons for the Return Home*, Wendt's first novel, and moves through chronologically to readings of *Ola*, *Black Rainbow* and the poetry collection *Photographs*. There have been subsequent publications, but since there has to be a cut off date, a retrospective bringing the reader up to the millennium seems appropriate. The study does a really fine job of making multi-cultural postcolonial global connections between Wendt's writing and that of fellow writers and critics. In terms of both theoretical framework and textual analysis, Sharrad's approach links Wendt's work to writers and critics such as Brathwaite, Borges, Wilson Harris, Ngugi wa Thiong'o, Fanon, Bhabha and Parry, while continuing to emphasize its association with popular culture.

That such a scrupulous general study has been made will enable future critics to focus for a while on specific issues of scholarship – the need for a more historicized, philosophically engaged reading of Wendt's textual relationship to existentialism, and the question of how such a reading might be compared with Samoan ideas and aesthetics, for example. It is surprising to find so little reference to Sina Va'ai's study *Literary Representations in Western Polynesia*, although it may be that because it is such a comprehensive and distinctive discussion in itself, the two studies can be read in conjunction. No book can answer all the questions; it would, however, be interesting to read more detailed historical analyses of the international effect of the politics of black power and civil rights on Wendt's writing.

Sharrad's discussion of the problem of situating *Leaves of the Banyan Tree*, Wendt's epic novel, in global literary terms, can be linked to the concluding suggestion that the diversity and skill of the literature of the Pacific region as a whole has not yet been accorded the international recognition it deserves because of a 'lag between production and significant reception'. This gap is about physical difference, time, distance, language, cultural specificity, and trends in genre that have rendered Wendt's reception as a global writer problematic. Sharrad, accurately in my view, reads this in terms of the productive locatedness of Wendt's writing. The discussion of differences between a language-based concept, such as Homi Bhabha's postcolonial reading of the third space, and va, a multivalent Samoan language term which concerns people-centered relations, is helpful in making such global/local distinctions apparent. They also show the importance of the interventions made by writers like Wendt in current literary developments. Discussions of how his work has influenced a younger generation of writers such as Teresia Teaiwa, Sia Figiel, and John Pule will be facilitated by Sharrad's study. Wendt himself celebrated the role of Pacific writers in the influential essay 'Towards a New Oceania' by explaining that 'In their individual journeys into the Void, these artists, through their work, are explaining us to ourselves and creating a new Oceania.' If Wendt's writing circles the void, then it is also connected to the universe of spirals where it will continue to exert an influence for a long time to come.

Briar Wood, London Metropolitan University

James Procter
Stuart Hall

Routledge Critical Thinkers London and New York: Routledge 2004
ISBN: 0 415 26267 4 pb 162pp £10.99

Helen Davis
Understanding Stuart Hall

London, Thousand Oaks, CA. and New Delhi: Sage Publications 2004
ISBN: 0 7619 4715 9 pb 222pp £16.99

Chris Rojek
Stuart Hall

(Key Contemporary Thinkers) Cambridge: Polity 2003
ISBN: 0 7456 2481 2 pb 230pp £14.99

The works of Stuart Hall have been helping to redefine the terrain of cultural inquiry for almost fifty years. Since 1957, when he abandoned his PhD thesis on Henry James, Hall has produced work on such varied fields as the post-war understanding of class; the popular arts; structures of codification in the media; youth subcultures; moral panics and draconian policing; the rise of Thatcherism and the crisis of the left; the 'New Times' project; identity politics and new ethnicities; and the complex character of multicultural Britain. His contributions have become central in many of these areas and the arguments found in the literature are often conducted within the terms of his input. Yet despite the amount of work he has produced (Chris Rojek's bibliography cites over ninety texts by Hall – even though it contains nothing from before 1970), Hall has never written a full-length, single-authored monograph and it remains difficult to reduce his manifold arguments to any single philosophy. If anything, his guiding principles would seem to be anchored in eclecticism, in contingency, and in the refusal of simple solutions to difficult problems. When Terry Eagleton in *After Theory* describes the later Hall as 'shifting decisively into the non-Marxist camp', the finality suggested by the term 'decisive' must surely give us pause. Hall's position, like the strain of Marxism he prefers, is always 'without guarantees'.

This is not to deny that there are consistencies across the decades of his writing and it is an achievement of each of these three studies to tease out and clarify the central intellectual cores of Hall's work. The debt to Antonio Gramsci's reformulation of the Marxist project is continually apparent in Hall's work since the 1970s but these books also trace the importance of the biographical parallels between the two thinkers. In locating both the lower-class Sardinian and the middle-class Jamaican on the margins of the dominant societal bloc, we can begin to see the roots of the conjunctural nature of each of their interventions into the political sphere. Each writer aims to produce specific strategies to address specific political problematics. The need for relevance to the task at hand can often trump the desire to produce a unified and complete theory and methodology of critical practice. For Hall, complexity must be addressed and, indeed, actively sought behind the obfuscating façade of common-sense ideologies. It is the resulting strategic and fragmented elements of Hall's work that most excite his champions and aggrieve his critics.

James Procter's book is the most suited to the reader in need of a complete introduction to Hall's work The text-boxes that provide information on such diverse topics as 'Mass Communications Research' 'Difference and *Différance*', 'Relative Autonomy', and 'Powell and Powellism' enhance Procter's account of Hall by locating his work within political, social, and academic trends. The student coming fresh to the field is well catered for by this background material. They would certainly be aided also by Procter's clear elucidation of Hall's own position, which is well supported by an inventive and accurate use of examples. The book is also useful for refusing to gloss over the breaks in Hall's thought. Instead it recognizes these as a necessary part of Hall's rejection of the possible institutionalization of cultural studies and the reification of his own role within the progress of that discipline. If there is a problem with Procter's text, it is in the fact that some important criticisms that can be made of Hall's work are subsumed within this catch-all conclusion. However, it is perhaps in the nature of an introductory text as this not to allow for an extended discussion of such material and, to give Procter his due, the interested reader is directed towards some of Hall's critics in the 'Further Reading' appendix.

Helen Davis's *Understanding Stuart Hall* is more concerned with defending Hall against his critics and certainly benefits from the author's own conversations with Hall (which are conveniently transcribed in the final chapter of this book). In particular, her unravelling of the complexity of Hall's association with *Marxism Today* and the 'New Times' venture is skilfully done and can go some way to releasing Hall from the charge of providing the theoretical groundwork for the Blairite assault on Labour Party ideology. However, her book is impaired by the occasional factual slip (such as the conflation of the Heysel and Hillsborough disasters) and a terrible quantity of typographical errors.

Rojek's book is the most complex and also the most critical. Rather than simply working through Hall's published writings in a roughly chronological order, he concentrates on opening up the reasoning behind Hall's central concepts, and examining systematically the coherence and importance of the articulations produced by Hall's interventions and borrowings from across the intellectual milieu. He carefully follows the dynamics of Hall's weaving between the monoliths of culturalism and structuralism, and perceptively notes each of the occasions when Hall's critics may find themselves on the stronger ground.

However, Rojek's conclusions are surprisingly non-committal and, in fact, echo worries voiced by Hall about his own intellectual labours. The commitment to difference is revealed as being inherently couched in negative terms. Rojek asks how a 'politics of hybridity' can succeed in 'establishing what different agents hold in common and building a strategy of transformation around binding political ends'. He argues that the success or failure of this project will vindicate or condemn much of Hall's life work. Yet Hall himself appears eminently aware of this and his quest to initiate a fruitful and productive sense of the politics of difference seems always to have been haunted by the spectre of the apolitical and futile 'kind of difference that doesn't make a difference of any kind'. His refusal to stop thinking and writing, and his insistence on continually challenging the cultural hegemony that would close down the possibility of democratic and liberating difference, are driven by this very fear.

Dave Gunning, University of Leeds

Peter Hallward
Absolutely Postcolonial: Writing Between the Singular and the Specific
Manchester: Manchester University Press 2001
ISBN 0 7190 6126 1   pb   433pp   £19.99

Absolutely Postcolonial by Peter Hallward attempts to move the criticism of postcolonial literature away from a politics of difference and location to a consideration of the aesthetics of contemporary fiction. The author's decision to examine postcolonial literature qua literature, while working with a specific understanding of the term postcolonial (which he carefully distinguishes from anti-colonial) is a refreshingly original contribution to the field, and has already won praise from such scholars as Paul Gilroy, Slavoj Zizek, and Diana Brydon. *Absolutely Postcolonial* first develops a concept of the singular, a non-relational category which, in contrast to the specific, generates its own terms of reference, based largely on Hallward's reading of Deleuze. The largest part of the volume is occupied with a reading of four contemporary writers, from the Caribbean, the United States, and Algeria: Edouard Glissant, Charles Johnson, Mohammed Dib, and Severo Sarduy, in whose work Hallward locates a tendency towards singularity.

While Hallward positions himself as a critic of postcolonial theory in general, those whom he takes to be representative of the field – Gayatri Chakravorty Spivak, Homi Bhabha and Aijaz Ahmad – have a variety of relationships to the term postcolonial, with the latter refusing to identify with it altogether. Indeed, Hallward both complains that the postcolonial is poorly defined, and draws on the established flexibility of the term in order to argue for the utility of reading otherwise disparate authors together and to advance his critique of the politics of location and territorialization. The volume's chief strength lies in its convincing demonstration of the futility both of demanding an ever increasing specificity in critical analyses of postcolonial texts, and in debating author's rights to particular subject matter.

The absence of work by female authors, coupled with the misogyny that Hallward himself identifies in some of the writers he has chosen, seems to point, however, to a need for the very identity politics which the volume refuses. Indeed, Toni Morrison and Assia Djebar, two women writers who are discussed in *Absolutely Postcolonial* appear only in the conclusion, as examples of specific writing; foils to the work of Charles Johnson and Mohammed Dib. Given that the author's readings of Glissant, Johnson, Dib, and Sarduy suggest that each writer undergoes a teleological development, beginning their careers with work that emphasizes location and progressing to create texts that embody a form of transcendentalism, the specificity of Morrison and Djebar seems, worryingly – if implicitly – to relegate them to an early stage of aesthetic development. Hallward's object is to help move postcolonial studies beyond its current focus on discourses of authenticity, and return to a version of universalism via an emphasis on the singular – singularities are, according to Hallward, necessarily 'self-universalising'. The possibility of a universalism which is not grounded in a specific culture or condition, however, still seems uncertain at the end of the book.

Anna Guttman, University of Leeds

Plant Care
Edited by E.A. Markham
Linda Lee Books 2004
ISBN 1 872659 03 9 pb 160pp £8.95

Unusually for a festschrift, *Plant Care* offers much to draw the reader in. On the evidence here, Mimi Khalvati has a passionate intelligence, is a much-loved stimulating teacher, fond of elephants, the sea, ice-cream, gardens, talking on the telephone, all things in miniature and red wine. A celebration of Mimi Khalvati's many contributions to poetry, and published to coincide with her 60th birthday, *Plant Care* is E.A. Markham's selection of tributes and poems from her friends, students, and literary admirers. It seems that along with her considerable talent as a poet, she has a real gift for friendship and many of the contributors recreate emotional memories about personal kindnesses and shared experiences.

Mimi Khalvati was born in Tehran and grew up from the age of six on the Isle of Wight. She went back to Iran at the age of seventeen, returning to England at twenty-five. She began writing poetry late, after a career in the theatre, publishing her first collection in her late forties. She has published five volumes of poetry with Carcanet Press, including her *Selected Poems* in 2000 and, most recently, *The Chine* (2002). She is also the founder and leader of The Poetry School, based in London, which offers a programme of tuition designed to encourage the writing and reading of poetry.

Plant Care opens with its best contribution: 'A Foster-tongue' by her publisher, Carcanet's Michael Schmidt. In it, he places her work in its contemporary context and outlines the reasons why her writing is so radical, so unusual, and so good. Khalvati has always written against the mainstream: she is best known for her formal, lexically adventurous poetry, her love of sequence: this is explained by Schmidt as 'the longing for scale and the need for a generous and inclusive complexity'. He writes that 'labels are retrospective and can be reductive' when describing her resistance to being placed into a particular ethnic category and this is an interesting insight into the struggle that the writer from a dual heritage has if she finds the labels confining.

Khalvati's work is first of all about language: Schmidt records her talking of how the effect of losing her first language, Persian, as a child, affected her relationship to her new language, English:

> to master this language was absolutely crucial. I also loved it, and I was good at it. ... I don't take it for granted, I'm not casual with it

In 'April the 28th Street', the best poem in the book, E.A. Markham describes her birthday as an address, distant now, once the scene of small battles, now 'flagged for celebration'. And so it is with this book, in which Khalvati's own voice is the strongest. It is testament to the editor's skill that this is so. The interview with her Italian translator, Eleonora Chiavetta, provides further insight into the workings of Khalvati's poetic imagination. Among the poems offered as tributes, many speak directly to her: *the café tables are laid out ready for Mimi* or *Dear Mimi* or *Your Tehran;* or they speak to and about her poems and their concerns: light, the natural world, elephants. There's rather a lot of carpet/fabric/tapestry, a nod to the Persian heritage. I especially liked Moniza Alvi's 'The Seconds' and Romesh Gunesekera's 'The Book': *there will be a party within/good wishes, colour and sound.* If you don't know her poetry, you may be left feeling like a gatecrasher at the party. You'll certainly need to know her work to fathom the meaning of some of the poems here. But that's no bad thing. Indeed, *Plant Care* is a useful companion to her work and certainly took me back to it. Not only is Mimi Khalvati one of the most interesting writers in these islands, she seems an awfully nice person as well.

Susan Burns, Chol Theatre, Huddersfield

Notes on Contributors

Born to a Dutch Burgher family in Sri Lanka, **Jean Arasanayagam** graduated from the University of Ceylon and the University of Strathclyde in Scotland. A novelist, poet, playwright, and artist, she is the author of over twenty books. Her wide-ranging themes include identity, inheritance, ethnicity, displacement, migration, and gender. She has won many local and international awards for her writing.

Robert Chandler has translated Sappho and Apollinaire for 'Everyman's Poetry'. His translations from Russian include Pushkin's *Dubrovsky*, Leskov's *Lady Macbeth of Mtsensk* and Vasily Grossman's *Life and Fate*. He has co-translated numerous works by Andrey Platonov; two of these – *Happy Moscow* and *Soul* – were shortlisted for the Weidenfeld European Translation Prize; another – *The Macedonian Officer* – won second prize in the 2004 John Dryden Translation Prize. 'Electrification' will be included in his edition of *Russian Short Stories: Pushkin to Buida* (2005).

Elizabeth Cook writes fiction, poetry and, most recently, a libretto. Her fiction *Achilles* was published in 2001. She is the author of *Seeing Through Words* – a study of late Renaissance poetry, and is the editor of the Oxford *John Keats*. She travelled in Russia with the help of a grant from the Author's Foundation.

Kai Easton, until recently lecturer in English at Rhodes University, is currently a Mellon postdoctoral fellow in English at the University of KwaZulu-Natal. A book on J.M. Coetzee is forthcoming.

Mick Gidley is Professor of American Literature at the University of Leeds. His recent work, including *Edward S. Curtis and the North American Indian Project in the Field* (2003), has been mainly devoted to Native American themes. His essay in this issue will appear, in different form, in his forthcoming book *Emil Otto Hoppe at Large: Photographing the Modern World*.

Shanaz Gulzar trained in Fine Arts at Leeds Metropolitan University and now works in theatre and digital media. She has been Associate Artistic Director of Chol Theatre, an arts and performance-led company, since 2002, and also continues working freelance.

Tajinder Singh Hayer is a writer based in Bradford, and currently teaches creative writing at the city's university. He has recently been a writer-in-residence at the West Yorkshire Playhouse in Leeds and will shortly be completing a play for that organization. The poems included here form part of a sequence which appears in E. Reiss, ed., *Through: Beehive Poets, Mirfield* (2004)

Karen King-Aribisala is an Associate Professor at the Department of English, University of Lagos, Nigeria. Her first book – *Our Wife and other stories* – won the Commonwealth Literature Prize 1990/91 for the best first book (Africa Region) and is being republished this year. Her second book, *Kicking Tongues*, was published in 1998/99. Her work has appeared in many journals including *Wasafiri*, *Bim*, and *The Griot*.

Subashree Krishnaswamy edited *Indian Review of Books* for a number of years. She also edited titles published under Manas, an imprint of East West Books (Madras). She is currently writing the Babel Guide to South Indian Fiction in Translation. She is also translating into English Tamil fiction written by women.

Dilip Kumar, whose mother tongue is Gujarati, is a well-known short story writer in Tamil with several awards to his credit. He has published two collections of short stories in Tamil. He has also edited *A Place To Live*, a volume of contemporary Tamil short stories translated into English (2004).

Gail Low teaches Contemporary Literatures in English at the University of Dundee. She has published widely on postcolonial literature in various journals, and is the author of *White Skins, Black Masks* (1996). She is presently researching an institutional history of 'Commonwealth Literature' in the UK, 1950-1965.

Padmini Mongia teaches literature in English at Franklin & Marshall College. She has published articles on Conrad, Arundhati Roy, and Amitav Ghosh, edited *Contemporary Postcolonial Theory*, and published poetry in *Catamaran, Ravishing DisUnities*, and *InvAsian*. She is currently working on a collection of short stories.

Water Stair (2000), **John Pass**'s most recent book, was shortlisted for the Dorothy Livesay Award (British Columbia Poetry Prize) and for Canada's most prestigious literary award, the Governor General's Award. Poems in this issue of *Moving Worlds* are from his fifteenth collection, *Stumbling In The Bloom*, due in 2005.

Geralyn Pinto is Senior Lecturer in English at St Agnes College, Mangalore, India. She recently submitted her Ph.D. thesis on narrative technique. She has written a number of long stories employing suspense, science fiction and the supernatural. A versatile actress, she has performed several times before the public of Mangalore.

David Richards is the Director of the Ferguson Centre for African and Asian Studies at the Open University. He is the author of *Masks of Difference: Cultural Representations in Literature, Anthropology and Art*. He is currently writing a book on modernism and archaeology.

Zahia Smail Salhi specializes in Arabic and Francophone literature, comparative literature namely the representation of Arab women in Orientalist discourse, and the literary expressions of Arab writers in the Diaspora. She works on gender issues in the Arab world, focusing on women, politics and the law, gender, and development in the Middle East and North Africa.

A poet and playwright who lives near Huddersfield, **Adam Strickson** has recently written 'Gods, Monsters and Body Ironing', a play about a Kurdish asylum seeker from Syria. His first full length collection of poetry, *An Indian rug surprised by snow*, will be published in December 2004.

Amina Yaqin is Lecturer in Urdu and Postcolonial studies at the School of Oriental and African Studies, University of London. She has written articles on women's poetry, language and communalism, and Pakistani culture. Her work in progress includes a monograph on Gender and Intertextuality in Urdu poetry.

CALL FOR PAPERS

The 29th Annual Conference of the
Society for Caribbean Studies
University of Newcastle Upon Tyne, UK
Wednesday 29 June – Friday 1 July, 2005

The Society seeks one-page abstracts, accompanied by a one-page CV, **by January 7th 2005** for research papers on the Hispanic, Francophone, Dutch and Anglo-Caribbean, and Caribbean disaporas. Papers can address the following themes, but we also welcome abstracts for papers, or full panel proposals, that fall outside the list of topics below. Authors of papers selected for the conference will be invited to give 20 minute presentations of their papers and offered the opportunity to publish their full papers on the society's web site.

PROVISIONAL PANELS

Children and childhood in the Caribbean, past and present
The sexual politics of Caribbean popular culture
Caribbean masculinities
Landscape and environment
Health and healing
Caribbean criminal justice
Democracy in crisis in the Caribbean?
The United States in the Caribbean
The Caribbean in the world economy
Comparative Caribbeanist research: A roundtable
Caribbean aesthetics
Visual culture
Amerindians in the Caribbean
Archives, museums, and public history
Memory, myth and narrative

The Society will provide a limited number of bursaries to postgraduate presenters, which will contribute to registration and accommodation costs, but not travel costs. **Postgraduate presenters should indicate that they are seeking a bursary when they submit their abstracts.** Arts researchers/ practitioners living and working in the Caribbean are eligible to apply for the Bridget Jones Travel Bursary, the deadline for which is **15 December 2004**.

Please send abstracts (one-page maximum, plus one-page CV), preferably by email, to the Chair of the SCS, Diana Paton, with 'SCS abstract 2005' in the subject line. For more information on the Bridget Jones Travel Bursary, contact Lynne Macedo.

Diana Paton
School of Historical Studies
University of Newcastle
Newcastle Upon Tyne
NE1 7RU
Diana.Paton@ncl.ac.uk

Lynne Macedo
Centre for Caribbean Studies
University of Warwick
Coventry
CV4 7AL
L.Macedo.1@warwick.ac.uk

For more information on the SCS see http://www.scsonline.freeserve.co.uk/carib.htm

Moving Worlds – 2005

Forthcoming issues:
5.1 Postcolonial Cities: Africa
5.2 Performing Arts in South Asian Literature